THE
MODERN
CAD GUIDE

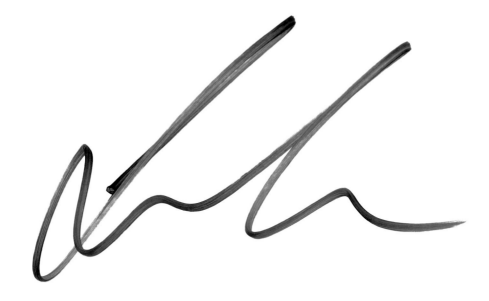

THE MODERN CAD GUIDE

Jaan Larner | Modern Cad Publishing

First Published in Great Britain 2006

Published by Modern Cad Publishing, a division of Modern Cad Limited, 8 Ipswich Road, Norwich, Norfolk NR2 2LP

Modern Cad Limited registered in England and Wales under Company Number 05544839

www.modern-cad.com

A CIP catalogue record for this book is available from the British Library

Cover design and typesetting by O2 Creative Limited

ISBN 0-9554611-0-3
ISBN 978-0-9554611-0-1

Printed and bound in Great Britain by Biddles Limited

Every effort has been made to contact and clear permissions with relevant copyright holders. Please contact publisher with any queries.

For everyone who made this book possible - good, bad and worse, you know who you are…

Contents

Welcome to the Modern Cad Guide ™

A guide to celebrate and recapture the fun and exuberance of a simpler time when men were men, women were women, and everyone actually had some fun.

The tide of political correctness has created generations of subservient men or loutish yobs - the former without character, the latter without charm.
Is it any wonder that women lament the passing of the charming and manly chap who would literally sweep them off their feet and into a waiting sports car, for a filthy weekend away?

So this guide was born to reinvigorate the legend of the rakish scoundrel, who squires ladies of incandescent beauty from bar to restaurant and hotel; a charming rotter who knows the taste of a perfect martini, the feel of a tailored suit and the way to a lady's heart.

We won't call, we don't do "nice" and we might sleep with your sister... but admit it you've missed us, haven't you…

The Cad

"Cad n.: a person who operates outside of societal norms: often characterised as having an ammoral outlook: unprincipled & morally reprehensible"

"Modern Cad n.: all of the above......but in a good way"

It is said that one must know the rules before one can break them, and the Modern Cad is the human embodiment of such an endeavour; He learns the rules to gain advantage, to be accepted as one of those in the know, to be accepted as People Like Us for the EXPRESS PURPOSE of breaking them. By seeming to behave by the rules, you encourage others to do the same.

Also it is often said that a gentleman is never unintentionally rude - and so it is with the Modern Cad - he is a gentleman in everything, except honourable intent - and sometimes even a Modern Cad can be persuaded to do the odd good deed, in fact in some cases, it is highly desirable.

However, there has been a decline in the number of true Cads and quality Cadmanship (being an adherence to the three pillars of Cad-dom: Charm, Confidence and Cunning).

With trainers, fast food, video games, new men, new lads and ladettes, the battlelines of social interaction have been progressively blurred, erased and shoddily redrawn.

Today, men are confused as to how they should behave; either take charge and be accused of being a chauvinist pig, a throwback and neanderthal – something of the '70s – or be solicitous, kind and generous, a principled fellow who would never cheat, never be late and never forget to wash up, Zzzzzzz – in short, a wimp; described with nauseating pity as a "nice" guy.

We might like to think that with boundless knowledge and emancipation for both sexes we could somehow tip the balance of relationships in favour of reason and accountability, but generations of male suffering and complaint, coupled with the hang-dog expressions on the faces of men up and down the country, offer a different prognosis.

However, in times past there were those, who in the darkest of times have been shining beacons of manly behaviour, who have led by example, eschewing the bleating complaints of the mediocre majority, daring to grasp at a life less ordinary: Oliver Reed, Ian Fleming, Terry-Thomas to name but a few.

This guide seeks to redraw the lines of the battlefield, to cut through the white noise of politically correct dogma, now as biased and oppressive as any pejorative language it sought to temper. To give back what has been lost to men everywhere and forge anew an ancient breed the Romans used to call Vir Venustus.

It will show you how to gain the upper hand by developing skills, cultivating attitudes and equipping you with tools that will leave you on top. Within this book you will learn the art, history, hallmarks and attitudes of the true Modern Cad.

Each chapter deals with a different skill, topic or body of knowledge that every Modern Cad should master.

You will learn the following and more:

- How to communicate and persuade with dastardly intent;
- How to master knowledge and deploy it to your caddish ends;
- How to belie your cunning and blend into any social setting;
- How to orchestrate your life and its contents to meet your sybaritic objectives;
- How to manage the Cad Continuum™
- Hard-won lessons in the art of seduction;
- How to be the envy of your peers; and
- The simplicity and power of the Cad Crumpet-Classification Cube™

By the end you will have a formidable arsenal at your disposal with which to tackle the world.
History is written by the winners of which you are one. A prince among men; a God among insects;

Claim your birthright…

Cad Skills & Knowledge

Here you will find a range of skills to develop and knowledge to acquire, which will give you the upper hand in all things Cad such as:

- phrasing that withering put down,
- choosing a suitably seductive restaurant,
- picking out the right loafers for slipping down a drainpipe

or

- whipping up a martini to sharpen the evening ahead.

As any field of human endeavour, it is subject to constant refinement and incorporation of the newest toy or latest social development. Therefore if you have any suggestions or comments please let us know at www.modern-cad.com. The skills and knowledge we cover in this section are:

- Cad Communication
- The Cosmopolitan Cad
- Cad Style
- Cad Cocktails

Cad Communication

"Language is the armory of the human mind, and at once contains the trophies of its past and the weapons of its future conquests" - Samuel Taylor Coleridge

"I wish people who have trouble communicating would just shut up" - Tom Lehrer

Introduction

There has been extensive research into communication skills and the Cadman should avail himself of any opportunity to learn more, as it equips him with his most formidable weapon in the daily battles of one's life.

Firstly, we look at the Anatomy of Conversation to understand the basics of what we are trying to do.

Next, given that the most common phobia is speaking in public, and the worry most people have in approaching a member of the opposite sex is that they don't know what to say, we suggest certain methods of building rapport, and thereby Being Winning.

Sometimes, of course, you will want to live up to the gentleman's maxim, which is to say, a gentleman is never unintentionally rude - therefore consider our proposals on Being Insulting.

Once in a position of having built rapport with those you wish to and dismissed those you do not, you will want to move onto the more advanced skills of Lying and its close friend, Apologising.

Lastly, we have a look at Miscellaneous other interesting items in the cad communications armory

Anatomy of a conversation

So before you take the stage, let's have a look at how we communicate.

Studies have suggested that communication is comprised of the following elements and in the following proportions:

	Face to Face	Telephone	Email/SMS/letter writing
Body Language:	55%	Ranges from 10-16%	10%
Tonality:	38%	approximately 70%	20%
Actual words:	7%	14% - 20%,	70%

Therefore be aware that your posture and how you modulate your speech is more important face to face than what you are saying — it might be relatively meaningless rubbish, but delivered confidently and with an engaging playful tone, they'll be eating out of your hand.

However, unsurprisingly, when you communicate purely by artificial means such as using text messages or email, the percentages are more skewed toward words – however your previous manner, body language and tonality will form an image in the mind of the reader which allows them to put what you say into context.

e.g., A dull man emailing a married woman saying "You adulterous whore" will get an entirely different reaction to the charming cad who is sleeping with her and emailing the same.

Therefore you should continue to flirt and play with your target via email in similar ways to how you spoke – but of course you can exercise more creativity and have more time to craft and hone a witty charming epic on email which will sweep her off her feet – especially effective with pseudo-intellectual foreign girls.

Body language
We assume you have a basic grasp of the English language and are able to differentiate between the tone of a playfully naughty murmur and a hostile growl. Body language is trickier. While there are some general rules, individuals vary and you have to place everything in context. For instance, crossed arms and legs usually indicate someone who is closed off and uninterested or even defensive - the room is unusually cold.

If you really want to become an expert ,we recommend almost anything by Desmond Morris or Derren Brown.

As a quick guide to female body language bear the following in mind (if any ladies are reading, you are experts at body language from birth so we won't bother to teach you to suck eggs - you can skip this section):

Signs she maybe interested:

- Dilated pupils (why do you think bars are dark?)
- Knees or feet pointed to you
- Body oriented towards you/leaning towards you
- Smiling
- Self-touching (hair, face, thighs etc)
- Lingering glances
- Complimenting you
- Touching you
- Moistening lips
- Cocked head
- Staring at your mouth

Caution
Do however be careful not to misinterpret these signs. Even in abundance they are not conclusive and can indicate other motivations. By way of example: One evening a Modern Cadman, was sitting in a bar with friends enjoying the company of a girl he had just been introduced to. She was to be a bridesmaid at an upcoming wedding of mutual friends and the MC was enjoying chatting and making increasingly flirtatious comments to the girl in question – she was pretty and attentive, nodding and smiling, often looking at his mouth, body oriented toward him and leaning forward, and frequently adjusting her hair, sweeping it behind her ears. "All systems go" thinks our hero, positive indicators galore, so he cruises in with a subtle "I'm

looking forward to seeing you at the wedding, but I do think we should have dinner first" – silence – then the girl said "Excuse me for a second" and got up to powder her nose – confused, the young MC turned to his chum, soon to be married at the forthcoming event, and explained this curious behaviour after such a catalogue of classic signs, only to be greeted with laughter. Eventually wiping the tears from his eye, the groom said "You daft twat, she's deaf. She was lip reading".

Being Winning

Your aim is to transform yourself in the eyes of the woman you are talking to from the dashing stranger to the exciting new lover.

Consider the following conversational gambits and make them feel at home with you.

Find out what makes them tick

People love to talk about themselves, especially in reference to happy times they have had or other high moments such as completing some challenge. So having established the following 3 things you should have no problem building up a conversational head of steam:

1   What is their passion?
2   If money were no object what would they do?
3   What are the most important lessons in life?

These questions answer who they are, where they are heading and what they have learned on the way. The last is especially important since it flatters them to be asked for their opinion on something unrelated to their station in life working equally well on waitresses or Heads of State.[1]

Anchor Positive Associations

Once you know what makes them tick, you can easily pick a topic which will get them thinking about a particularly happy or satisfying moment in their lives. This in turn associates you with that moment and that feeling of being happy or even aroused. This is good news. They already have a positive opinion of you. However, you can go further and anchor that association with a phrase ("Fantastic!", "You're so right"), gesture (lighting a cigarette, proposing a toast or even just smiling broadly) or tactile movement (touching their arm or hand), or a combination, for maximum effect. You can then recreate those feelings in the person you are talking to at any time you meet afterwards, by repeating the anchoring device.

Occasionally overload and then throw in a life-line

This is only to be used sparingly, but sometimes it is useful to rapidly cover a topic you know well, demonstrating your easy mastery of it. This makes the listener feel uninformed or simply impresses them and leaves them a little lost giving them a lifeline to re-enter the conversation. This is especially effective when the topic appears to be suggested by someone else and for which you could have not prepared. A useful technique is the "Three most important things" ploy referred to in the Cad Seduction section which uses the minimum of effort to deliver the maximum effect.

Politicians use this often, ending a stream of statistics or other dullness with a memorable soundbite, which the audience in their relief carry away with them.

As a side note, statistics are very useful; most people are scared of numbers and faced with a stream of them, followed by something intelligible, they hang onto the last part. e.g. "recent studies show that the incidence of statistical misunderstandings grew from 43% in written discourse to over 75% in everyday conversation – in short, if you're going to bull shit; do it face to face".

[1] Do, by the way, let us know if you do manage to seduce a head of state – we've got a friend who'd love to swap notes.

Be honest and direct

There are some people who can say exactly what's on their mind and have it come true.

Examples:

Chap [walking up to the bar and a woman he hasn't met before] "So are you going to buy me a drink?"
Chappess "..Only if you pay for the cab home..."
This is an example of a cad and a caddette recognising each other and wasting no time.

Another wordier approach, might be this:

"We have now reached the part of the evening where convention dictates that that I ask you to come back to my place – now, of course, I know that if I do ask you, you will be bound to say 'no' for reasons of chastity, propriety and, frankly, being a nice girl – whereas, if I don't ask, you will be offended and think I don't find you attractive – so can we take it as read that I have asked you, that you have said no and get on with our evening?"

Both encounters required a double occupancy cab-ride home within minutes - and another the next morning.

If you are this sort of person, and you know who you are, good luck to you. You lucky bastards...

Be Positive

Don't use questions that expect a negative answer, like "I don't suppose you'd like to go out would you?" Instead, say with a smile "We should have dinner".

The former is too easy to turn down, even if she would quite like to have dinner. Such a miserable plea, dripping with insecurity almost demands a slap down – the latter is a challenge, "Prove me wrong, we should have dinner"

Be general

Having found out what makes someone tick, it should be easy to deliver a slightly tailored generalisation that could apply to almost anyone, which the recipient takes as a singular insight into who they are or more importantly who they want to be seen to be.

> I'm sure people always ask your opinion about things....
> Do people find your confidence a bit overwhelming?
> I'm sure you never have a problem being direct, but...

or taking another tack, hint at some common frustration:

> Do you ever get frustrated that your insights are overlooked?
> You come across as very confident, but there's a shyness too, isn't there?

Flatter their intelligence

Good looking people want to appear smart and with smart people it's often all they've got, so flatter the recipient's intelligence - praise their insight, ask their opinion, re-interpret a comment of theirs in the best possible light, and above all, look impressed that they are up to YOUR standard.

Being Insulting

Very often someone crosses your path who is just crying out to be insulted - either because they have insulted you or because you want to put them on the back foot for some reason.

Therefore, while a gentleman is never unintentionally rude, a cad is never without a withering put down.

Insults range in value and effect:

Blatant and upfront
"I'm sleeping with your wife" at a dinner party hosted by the cuckold or simply "you're a c**t" almost anywhere in public except certain trading floors, where it is practically a term of affection.

Localised
Delivered one to one, but without witnesses - either because there are none or because they don't pick up on the insult - usually using a term of art or jargon only known to the pair of you e.g., "so if you work really hard will they make you a barrister?" to a solicitor.

Subtle
The recipient doesn't realise that he is being insulted, but everyone else does. e.g. "Neat job, Mr Prescott"

For an extended masterclass in scornful insults, see almost every of the episode of Blackadder.

Lying

Or "Creative falsehood in the face of preferred alternatives or damaging revelations."

Broadly there are two reasons for lying:

1   because of something you have done; or
2   because of something you are about to do

Because sometimes the truth is too unpalatable for the recipient's ears.

You don't need a law degree to be good at lying; just a brazen attitude and the moral outlook of a weasel.

Something you have done (or not)
This begins with "the dog ate my homework" and ends with "I did not have sexual relations with that woman".
If you don't care, you may not even have to lie - Simply brazen out the truth:
"So you weren't ill, when you called in sick?"
"Nope - I skipped off to a stag weekend in Prague to get ripped off my tits in lapdancing bars."
"Oh".

Otherwise there is usually some advantage to maintaining even a flimsy pretext to cover for your behaviour - often this is because:

a)   You need to maintain the status quo - telling the woman whose house you live in that you have been like a rat up a drainpipe while away on "business" is not smart - flowers and complaining of how hard you had to work while away, is.
b)   You want to avoid censure or penalty: This may be due to some minor infringement of some obscure penal code "So when did you start exporting arms to terrorists in exchange for drugs?", "I have no clear recollection of the matter to which you refer, Senator" or some unfortunate but entirely innocent accident "No, I can't imagine how the burglar managed to get away with your entire collection of plush toys, only to incinerate them on the barbeque as he fled, without damaging any of the doors, windows or locks..."
c)   You want to reap the rewards of your cunning or gain some advantage "If you promised me that you would never die I would make love to you right now...", "I promise...I will never die" (thanks to Team America). Maybe you will need to take credit for someone else's work in the office ("Yes, I was surprised how much I knew about Cost Based Accounting too..."), discredit a rival ("That's right... he slept with my mother"), or should your life run in more rarified circles, at Court ("people should be pampered or utterly destroyed"`).
d)   You feel like it.

Something you are about to do

Imagine the situation. You have in good faith accepted an invitation from a sturdy and solid friend, only to have the chance to go to something much better arise in the meantime.

Your approach depends on a) your relationship with the recipient and b) the disparity between the options.

If you had, say, arranged to meet a chum for a beer, but had subsequently been invited to go skiing with the Storm Modeling Agency, all expenses paid for the weekend, no friend worth speaking to would mind you blowing them out. However, if the event is on a par with the original plan socially speaking or ostensibly "lower" socially or financially, then you may have to lie. Blowing out a bloody awful wedding full of harridans and twats vs. going to a bar with some mates might appear to the bride and groom to be rude - but what can you expect from such dull little people.

Planned	Preferred alternative	Acceptable?
Wedding	Beers, another wedding	No
Beers	Beers	No
Beers	Wedding, skiing with supermodels	Oh Yes

Therefore, if you are sadly without such an invitation, but need to get out of a pressing engagement consider the following:

Overwhelming Fate or Gross Incompetence

You need to demonstrate that you'd love to see your chum for a few ales/ go to the dreadful union/ bore yourself rigid at some mewling spawn's christening, but that pressure of an overwhelming sort is being applied to you. This might take the form of:

1   guaranteed sex with some nubile hotty which will earn his grudging respect while he calls you a CSV (which will make him feel better about you bailing on him),

2   the pressure of familial ties (you need to assist your ageing 'rentals, who are a bit infirm these days etc etc. with some heavy lifting, thorny problem etc), or

3   an accident outside of your control requiring your urgent attention, e.g., vital work deadline, boiler explosion at home, flooding, plague, pestilence etc

We have found that adding an element of personal inconvenience adds a convincing gloss to even the most steaming pile of ex-culpatory ordure.

Alternatively, fall on your sword by honestly (-ish) saying that you have been a villager and double booked yourself - tickets for the theatre bought by the bird at great personal expense, am a nob, but can we change date? This is particularly effective with male recipients of the news, since they will at least be rational - women can be annoyed in the face of any rational reason - Fault is not a necessary precursor to blame for the female of the species. Therefore stating to most men that you have made a mistake will set that seal on the truth of your statement, since why would any self-respecting red-blooded male admit such a lapse in ability and lower his status publicly, unless it was true? They feel superior and believe you - in fact they may feel subconsiously that they owe you for making them feel better about their own abilities.

Of course, you have a complete fund of self-respect - that's how you can do it. Only insecure people cannot take criticism, even if directed inwards.

Timing and overwhelming fate

Different approaches will require different timing - telling him you are having a boiler explosion on Friday is more than slightly odd, if today is Tuesday and it is no good having the boiler go on the Tuesday, you'd have it dealt with by Friday. Alternatively other excuses have a nice lead time to them (some work crises, deaths in the family, going to jail etc). Therefore kill off the relative beforehand or blow up the house on the day. The closer it is to the time of the meeting, what you lose in consideration for breaking the engagement, you gain in apparent veracity. Conversely, the sooner you break it off, the less egregious the breach, but the more calculated it will appear.

Occams Razor Approach to Creative Falsehood

The simplest answer is often the best and most convincing, especially if combined with judicious use of the most powerful convincing agent in the world - "The Truth".

Offering three reasons why you can't go smacks of trying hard to get out of it - a dead grandmother, a car crash and the pressure of work would seem over the top. So go for one simple one, but remember that unless your family have significant polygamy issues or you live in Lincolnshire, you should have no more than 2 sets of grandparents to kill off.

Demeanour

You need to sell the argument - much easier if you are using email, since you don't actually have to act and sound convincing down the phone, much less face to face. However again, what you gain in convenience, you lose in apparent veracity and vice versa.

In order of increasing cowardice and convenience:

- Face to face
- Phone call
- Email
- Text message
- Letter
- Carrier pigeon

Getting someone else to do it

Whatever approach you use, express your disappointment with emotion (bear with me, chaps) - annoyance, sadness, resignation, or even anger. You need to convey the idea that this is more inconvenient for you than it is for them. You can emphasis the cost by saying something like: "I haven't been out for ages and was really looking forward to it - or even more powerfully "I haven't seen you for ages and was really looking forward to it" (this may or may not ring true depending how well the subject knows him/herself).

Conviction

No, not the kind you get at Bow Street magistrates after that night on the Absinthe - It is important to be convinced of what you say and deliver it as a fait accompli - there should be no shilly-shallying around - you can't make it and that's that, but you can another time, bang, done. People respect authority and decisiveness, so go in confidently.

Re-arrangement as necessary

This is crucial and, frankly, only good manners - You should always offer alternative dates to meet up. Not only does this salvage something, mitigating the sting of cancellation, it makes your excuse more compelling because you clearly do want to meet up. It is important to take care of their ego

Apologising and other forms of insincerity

The first thing you need to understand about apologising is that it has nothing to do with being in the wrong - it is all about making the recipient of your apology feel superior and in the right.

A simple "I'm sorry" is effectively an admission to the person you say it to that they are somehow better than you.

A more complex apology can show affection and effort and places you higher in the pecking order than any other poor slob vying for her attention. Consider this classic trinity of Apology, Admission and Admiration *[her thoughts in square brackets]*

I'm sorry *[hmm... a good start]*. I was wrong *[well, I knew that]*, I love you *[Ha! Got him back under control]*

- Unbeatable.

Be creative and avoid cliches - and if you must buy flowers, do so for no reason, not just because you've actually done something wrong.

Miscellaneous Observations on Communicating

It has been said that to communicate effectively it is not enough to be understood - you must be incapable of being misunderstood. Well, lawyers and other dullards will trot that kind of crap out at every opportunity to justify their anally retentive personalities and fees. However, Cads live in the grey and shadowy realms of misunderstanding and thrive on mistaken belief. Therefore a cunning cad linguist should be prepared to be vague. Of course, being English helps enormously since the language was practically designed to be equivocal, with so many phrases open to interpretation.

The phrase "Well Quite" and its innumerable uses

When you are stuck for something to say – unusual, but not unheard of – you will seldom find that you cannot use a well delivered "Well quite". By subtly adjusting your tone you can respond in a satisfactory manner as far as the listener is concerned without conveying any information at all, but seemingly communicating that you have a thorough grasp of his or her point. This may be because you agree, but wish to reserve your position, you disagree, but don't want to overtly offend (yet) or because you haven't the faintest idea what they just said:

Tired?	Well…. Quite (as in "Not too tired, no…")
I like bunnies and want to work for world peace	Well quite (as in "This shouldn't take long…")
"So if we assume x to equal Phi, and relate it to the rest of the physiognomy of the subject one might conclude that the symbology of a number of societies which, while having superficial similarities, are in fact related by a coincidental discovery of a universal constant rather than by any direct propagation of societal or artisitic norms."	Well quite (as in "No idea what you just said, but I want to agree in the hope that you won't try and explain it to me any further, you dull little man")
I find bear baiting, cock fighting and seal clubbing entirely agreeable set of pastimes	Well quite (as in "Of course you do, you repulsive excuse for a human being")

Brevity and Colloquialisms we like:

SNAFU: Situation Normal: All Fucked Up
In a bar, empty wallet, no chums in immediate vicinity.

TARFU: Things Are Really Fucked Up
Her husband comes home early and drunk, and you are faced with a choice: get dressed and face him like a gentleman or shin down the drainpipe naked, without your wallet or keys.

FUBAR: Fucked Up Beyond All Recognition
You walk out of the private booth in a Croatian strip joint to find your boisterous 16 fellow stags have all left, without paying, after an altercation over the bill and happened to accidentally punch one of the strippers on the way out, leaving you to face the music as the 4 ex-army bouncers turn to see you walk in…

Cosmopolitan Cad or
"The Wherewithal to Survive Wherever"

"I have only two ambitions in life: one is to drink every pub dry... and the other is to sleep with every woman on Earth" - Oliver Reed

The Cad-about-town is an enviable fellow, who has at his fingertips, an encyclopaedic knowledge of cool bars, exciting restaurants, discreet hotels and other venues of note.

He is welcomed almost everywhere by staff in the form of doormen, barkeepers, concierges and maitre d's, for whom he may adopt a range of personalities and guises appropriate to the venue - the foppish sloane, the serious professional, the exuberant entrepreneur

We shouldn't forget the many events, parties and other happenings that crop up throughout the year, in which the Modern Cad should immerse himself.

Finally, he is equally at home whether near home or in far flung places.

Opening a new bar, club or restaurant? Let us know, we'll review it and let our members know by sending the details to: www.modern-cad.com

Venues

General points about all venues:

Preparation   Always do your homework – knowing your way around a venue is invaluable and if that extends to the staff even better. Whether this consists of knowing amusing anecdotes (essentially who drank, slept, ate, shagged or died there) or simply knowing where the bar is ("follow me"), you will feel more confident if you can demonstrate an intimate knowledge of the venue, and more importantly, have it noted by your companions. Your status will be enhanced in the eyes of women and men will be impressed or, better still, intimidated, especially if you are better-known to the staff of a venue they themselves know well.

So if you are going to a new venue, turn up early or some days before, to do a recce and if possible meet the staff (see below).

Also pay attention to the surrounding venues, so if you need a) an onward venue to continue the carousing, b) an escape route from someone or something dull, violent or embarrassing or c) need to spirit your soon to be new best friend away for a more intimate chat you can take charge and lead the way in confidence

Selection   You can't possibly keep track of every venue, so use the advice of people you trust or a well-tested guide book (hmm, there's an idea). Ensure that whoever you take advice from has the same taste and standards as you. I'm sure some people think Yates Fighting Pubs, sorry… Wine Lodges, are great fun, but I'll stick with the Lanesborough, if you don't mind.

Expectations   Never be afraid of asking for exactly what you want. The world is an imperfect place, mistakes are made and you are a busy chap. Rooms are misallocated, champagne isn't chilled and sometimes it turns out she isn't that sort of girl after all. Avoid all that wasted time and unpleasantness by being concise and upfront about what you expect from the start.

Standards   Never feel tied to a place. You should not feel that simply because you were invited somewhere that you have to stay – Once again, Life is short: too short to spend with dull people, cheap wine and ugly surroundings. And don't feel the need to apologise either – just go. Your disappearance will probably be considered mysterious and enhance your reputation for intrigue. Or they'll think you're rude and arrogant, which is a major turn-on too.

Timing   Never be early – this should be instinctive – if you are early you clearly haven't got somewhere better to be or have been.

Rapport   Always try and build rapport (see Cad Communication) – whether this is with your companion or the staff. If you talk to a person about themselves, they will listen for hours and adore you. All the while, you should be asking open questions which will provide considerable information for you to store away for use next time you want an 'in' (if necessary make notes in your little black book – this can even be incorporated in a little role-play – who wouldn't want to be interviewed?)

There is nothing wrong with asking the name of the person serving you, so long as you do so politely – it can even get them to lift their game since you could be from head office or looking for someone to complain about or compliment to the management.

Then use the name often – firstly, it creates familiarity and secondly, it will help you remember it. You might even hear the staff member's name mentioned before you meet them, which is even easier. Use it then and since they meet hundreds of people they will simply assume you have already been introduced. The only exception to this principle is if they have a name badge – using their name without an introduction just shows you can read…

Consistency

Play the long game. Don't try to become the favourite regular instantly. Relentless incremental improvement, however small, can build into a strong relationship which will stand you in greater stead than an all-out charm offensive.

Generosity

Always look after the little guy. They have tough jobs dealing with charmless and arrogant people all day and night. Rise above the tiresome mob by being the decent guy, especially in the smarter bars (boorish behaviour seems to increase almost exponentially with the size of people's wallets or, more likely, daddy's – not that they don't have their uses…). Like the Rat Pack, tip like a king, but do it in private and buy the guys a drink – with a bit of luck and over time, they will remember you and serve you first which a) saves time and b) always impresses (especially if it is with a "Hi! Great to see you. Your usual martini? And for your beautiful friend?")

Hotels

"Hotels are to adults what bus shelters are to teenagers." — AA Gill

Whether you are staying for a week or an hour (it is important to check the hotel policy on short stays) a hotel exists to service your needs in a way that you could not afford without a personal staff of butlers, maids and chefs. Generally they are also smarter than where you live and have the crucial benefit of being filled with people who have no idea who you or your companion are.

Since the hotel staff are there to minister to your every need, you should be ready to take advantage. A thoughtful bottle of champagne pre-ordered, chilled and waiting in the room is simple to arrange and sets the right tone.

This is especially impressive if you have only just turned up on a spur of the moment whim.

The Concierge

This is arguably the most important person in the hotel (apart from you). They can arrange anything from a taxi to a personal massage (sometimes simultaneously) and you need only ask. Assuming you are staying at one of the smarter hotels (where else?) the concierge will also have contacts in the local nightclubs, casinos and restaurants and get you on to their guest-lists for the duration of your stay. Played correctly, one night in a smart hotel can ensure that you are on the mailing lists of all the major clubs in the vicinity; add some well-aimed chat, make some donations to the charity of the doorperson's choice and you can make sure you jump the queue whenever you come back.

It has even been known for people to impersonate guests they know to be staying simply to call in with the name and room number and get the concierge to set them up with passes to the best clubs. They're in the wrong name, but that can be handy too...

Upgrades

The height of the art would be to walk into a smart hotel lobby like James Bond, dripping wet dressed only in pyjamas and a year's unkempt beard growth, and still be welcomed like a valued guest. Presumably, with the weight and credit of MI6 behind you, this is not so much of a chore, but we can't all rely on such largesse from our employers or the British taxpayer; more's the pity.

Like dealing with any business, you have to appeal to the profit motive – it must be in their interest to treat you well or at least better than any random schmo off the street. Therefore, consider being a little entrepreneurial. The Hotel's interest is in getting valuable consideration for all the empty rooms they have. If they are fully booked you have no chance and will simply have to pay the going rate. If not and they like you, you can be at the negotiating table.

Essentially you want to get the most for your money, by encouraging the hotel to part with things that cost it as little as possible, because it sees a benefit either immediately or in the long run.

Example #1 If you are in charge of where 10 of you on a stag weekend are staying, then you can encourage the hotel to upgrade you to get the booking (whether you keep this benefit for yourself or spread it around is up to you).

Example #2 Organise a birthday or other celebration (better yet a charity function – no-one likes to be seen to be uncharitable) at the hotel bar and ask for a room or bonus drinks/food in exchange for bringing the 50-100 people to spend a lot of money in their bar – and they will spend a lot in the bar; they're your friends, after all.

Remember it is always easier for them to add items to an existing order for the same money than agree to charge less for the same amount. So expect to get another room at a discount or free when you hire the suite at midnight, rather than a discount on the room itself, although there is no harm in trying.

Example #3 Promoting a venue can often encourage a hotel to be generous – therefore any hotel which would like to be featured on the Modern Cad guide please let us know and send details of your in-room cocktail list.

Ingratiating yourself

As well as appealing to their wallets, being a gregarious and charming chap, you will doubtless have your fair share of invitations to join people at chic venues – therefore, whether it is a wedding, corporate presentation or birthday party, see how many of the following people you can meet:

- The manager
- The night concierge (he or she usually has more scams running and so is better connected and informed than the day concierge)
- The bar manager and staff
- The maitre d'
- The housekeeper

Note down their names, cultivate their friendship, be decent, funny and wise – and tip well.

These people are in charge of the scarce resource you want and are in a position to make your stay exceptionally better.

Last minute bookings

A hotel around midnight with rooms to spare has an air of desperation about it – press home your advantage by asking for the most outrageous discount imaginable – and then swap it for a very good upgrade.

Restaurants

Restaurants may be judged in many ways. However, the Modern Cad has simple criteria. He looks for somewhere:

Enjoyable / Intimate / Discreet

The quality of the food and service should be suited to the occasion, whether a dinner for 2 or a birthday party for 30. The surroundings should match the mood you are trying to achieve and you will want no interruptions or any prying eyes.

Such seclusion can be difficult to find, but your efforts will be rewarded.

Obviously the smarter, the restaurant the more difficult it will be to get in, so how do you make it past the sneering derision of the minimum wage jobsworth on the telephone? The 'Abe Froman technique' is effective, but not for beginners, therefore you should rely on preparation, flexibility and mendacity:

Preparation   Take a leaf out of the investment banking world – many investment banks will have people who, while their day job is ostensibly to sell shares, fiddle with spreadsheets or whatever, have a remit to entertain blue chip clients by night. To do so, money is not enough, so they have their PA call every Monday to book tables as early as they can for all the best spots, sometimes up to a year in advance. Getting a table at the Ivy in a year isn't so bad, it's in half an hour on a Friday night, that's tricky. This way, the exhausted broker can entertain his client anywhere they want, any day of the week. This can also work with bars and clubs.

Flexibility   Be flexible on time and they may be able to help you, but don't expect to be dining in the prime evening slots between 7.30 and 9.30. Also being on stand-by for cancellations can reap benefits, but often this is simply a ruse to get you off the phone.

Downright lying   This requires some chutzpah, but call the restaurant saying you are PA to a VIP and are looking to book tonight, but importantly do not try and actually book it – just say you are looking for space, ask about security, exits, other diners, familiarity with celebs etc, but don't say who it is. Then tip off the paparazzi that, say, Robbie Williams, will be dining there. Finally call the restaurant an hour later to book in the name of "Mr Williams". Often the papers will have called to confirm that he is there, which will alert the booker and add weight to your claim. This assumes, of course, that the manager is not actually on speaking terms with Robbie William's PA, but you pays your money and you takes your chances. By the way do make sure the VIP in question is both in the country and, importantly, alive.

The Maitre d' and waiting staff

The manager of a restaurant is a person with a difficult job – they need to fill their restaurant with high ticket, low maintenance customers who will spend quickly and leave before dawn. It is often the case that in turning up and ordering your pre-dinner drinks you are greeted with a much friendlier welcome than you expected from the diffident and borderline suicidal receptionist. How come?

Well, it is a reasonable bet that having noticed that you are spending on pre-dinner drinks, what most people spend on dinner and choosing sensibly, but not ostentatiously, from the wine list, the maitre d' recognises a chance to cultivate a cash cow.

You may even find that the table you were expecting in the back, next to the kitchen is no longer appropriate and instead you are given pride of place.

Appealing to their wallets in a more direct manner can also be highly effective. However be careful not to embarrass them in doing so. Heaven forbid that their façade of aloof civility and masterful control should be marred by the implication that they handle something as grubby as cash. Therefore, so that they can save face and ego, the carefully folded note extended in the hand of friendship should, if the paper has been sufficiently difficult to fold, be enough to ensure that it is greeted in the manner it has been proffered.

So basically impress them or bribe them, it amounts to the same thing.

As for the waiting staff, apply the same approach you would with anyone who serves you. You need them more than they need you and they don't have soup for you to spit into.

Bars and Clubs

Bars, pubs and clubs are great places and the natural habitat of the jobbing Modern Cad. They are usually heavy with expectation and the buzz of pre-coital excitement . Depending on where you drink they may smell like cheap perfume and desperation or Chanel and money, but let's be under no illusion, they fulfill the same basic functions:

- To allow you to see and be seen
- To meet members of the opposite sex
- To get ripped off your tits for almost any reason
- To relax with friends or colleagues

Classifications of bars merge into one another so as to defy perfect description. Is it better to be in a classic country pub, with roaring log fires, supping ale with hearty locals in muddy wellies and chunky jumpers, than drinking martinis in a smart city bar mixing with the suited and moneyed?

The answer is that it depends on your mood and what you are trying to achieve. Whether you are chasing 18 year old nymphets/sharp suited business women/game country lasses to where they roam or are wolfing around in your local hostelry of choice, it doesn't matter so long as you adapt to your surroundings – Hunters and dog-slobbered-tweed are as welcome in the City as polished brogues and a Blackberry are in a country pub.

Professional attention

As a dapper Cad-about-town you may attract the attention of certain women of 'negotiable affection' – they will naturally be drawn to your aura of power and wealth much the same way as other women, but will expect to be paid well for their attention. While we would never want to dictate what may or may not be deemed acceptable, nor encourage any criminal activity, the individual cad's response is naturally entirely up to him. We only mention it so that you may be prepared and unsurprised if and when the conversation turns to the price of more than the drinks.

Getting in the door

Bit of a chicken and egg situation here – your best way to improve your chances of getting into a venue in the absence of membership, a friend who is a member or being on a guest-list, is to develop a relationship with the door staff once you are inside, but unless you have a relationship, how do you get in? – Well, use those special parties and guest-lists and the well-known friend. Then once inside get to know all the door staff:

Door hostesses

This can be difficult as they are practically immune to all advances – they fend them off all the time and from far richer, better looking and more famous people than you. So you need to seem like you a) aren't trying to chat them up b) know the venue and c) don't expect to be turned away – in fact you don't even try to get in. Whatever happens, don't hang around like a desperate groupie at a boy band gig – saunter up confidently and say "Hi I'm due to meet some friends here later, I just wanted to check they were on the guest list" –This works because you are clearly not trying to get in and you are asking for the benefit of others, thus distinguishing you in the eyes of the hostess as "Someone different"- when, of course, your friends are not on the list (how could they be? they've never even heard of this club) say "Well that's no good; Amex concierge were supposed to have sorted this out." – then ask "Who are they supposed to have called?" – instant conversation, which flatters her "expertise" and avoids you looking like a letch.

Male door staff

Usually of the large and sinister variety, so assuming that's not your kind of thing, see if there is some common ground you can establish – they may be ex-military – in which case you ask "when were you 'in'?" – this usually cues a conversation about whether you were and you should make suitably noises about "Nothing serious but I did a bit when I was younger" and refer to some mates who are still "in".

Also bear in mind that casually wandering up and asking to make a suitable donation to the charity of the doorman's choice often goes a very long way…

Events

The Season is an exciting time and the draw of Cartier, Ascot, Wimbledon, Henley and Cowes all exert their draw on the well-heeled, or at least well-connected, Cad-about-town.

All promise the chance for the beautiful, and possibly wealthy (certainly highly leveraged), to drink champagne in the sun under the pretence of watching some sport or other entertainment. You can guarantee that most participants haven't picked up or gripped an oar, racket, mallet, crop or mainsheet in years, if ever, and couldn't tell a divot from a drop shot. This hardly matters, of course, since it is all about seeing and being seen. Not to mention getting whammed on Pimms and into each others' pants.

Getting in

It is well known that the wealthy and famous are often given those things for which mere mortals have to pay. The trick therefore is to skip from one classification to the other by dint of cunning, luck or sheer brazen audacity, unless you have the means or the right chum in the right place – in which case you can send the tickets to Cad Towers (contact us at freestuff@modern-cad.com). Once again, confidence is vital and there are worse ways of gaining entry to an exclusive venue than by striding forward and casually saying "They're with me" and waving to the glamorous group following you into the enclosure.

Once in, half of your normal work is done for you. Everyone inside assumes that you are supposed to be there and their guard is lowered. You merely need to maintain a sufficient facade to preserve the illusion.

Be careful however, not to seem too grateful or ingratiating – aloof and slightly bored-looking is the demeanour you're after – you've been there, seen it and got the silver martini glasses in a presentation gift case.

A quick run down a couple of the more enjoyable events:

Cartier Polo
Cartier Polo Smiths Lawn

What: International polo event - Once upon a time it would have been rather sloany with a serious interest in the Polo matches, but most people turn up to get drunk in the China White tent to celeb-spot, while avoiding the interior designers from some dreadful makeover show. Usually held on the last Sunday in July.

Where: Guards Polo Club, Smiths Lawn, Windsor, England.

Who: Huge breadth - Royalty from the Queen on downwards, A list celebrities to Z list Big Brother mutants, Russian mafia dolly birds in diamante fuck-me pumps and ex-public school kids breaking up the boredom of their summer holidays spent temping in London before getting into an Oxbridge-reject university like Exeter, Bristol or Durham. Oh and one or two high class hookers…

How: Anyone can buy a ticket, just go here www.guardspoloclub.com/tickets – or you could get someone to go into the members section and bring out a few of the members tabs – they don't often check once you're in.

Tactics: get a team to drive down in an old Range Rover (will fit in perfectly), park up next to a couple of Ferraris or Bentleys and have a picnic before wandering up past the rather smart stands offering anything from bespoke hats to tickets to win a DB9 to drive in the Gumball 3000. Blag your way in or buy a ticket into the members' enclosure - Have a couple of drinks while watching the polo in the main stand – the commentaries are excellent and often hilarious. Say hi to the Queen if you see her and carry on drinking and schmoozing until early evening when you decamp to the China White tent. We recommend taking the following day off…

Dress-code: Anything from smart suits, blazers, panamas and chinos to jeans and a t-shirt – very egalitarian – many of the ladies will dress up in summer frocks, Jackie O glasses and high heels, before tottering onto the pitch between chukkas to tread the divots; hopefully without falling over or spilling their champagne.

Henley
Henley Royal Regatta

What: International rowing event drawing crews and oarsmen from all over the world – a week of successive knock-out events culminate in the finals of over the weekend. End of June/early July

Where: Henley upon Thames, England

Who: A mix of corporate types entertaining clients and ex rowers bedecked in garish rowing blazers and boaters. This is a genuinely elite sporting event so you see a mix of sports celebs, such as Sir Steve Redgrave, James Cracknell and a host of rowing internationals. Keep an eye out for the ongoing feud between Leander Club and the Black Sheep Rowing Club – one a venerable and elite rowing club on the Henley course, the other a virtual rowing club comprised of occasional, but generally ex rowers whose oarsmanship is matched only by their prodigious drinking ability – sponsored by the Black Sheep brewery in Masham.

How: If you only want access to the general or regatta enclosure go here to download an application form http://www.hrr.co.uk/downloads/downloads.asp. If you want to get anywhere interesting and more exclusive you will have to cultivate someone with some clout and preferably someone with a Full Metal Jacket – For a very entertaining and informative essay on the entire event, where to go and how to get in, go to http://www.twrc.rowing.org.uk/hrr/henleyguide.htm

Tactics: You could get away with having no knowledge of rowing at all, but try and feign some as it will make the day easier in case you meet a real boatie. You should especially be trying to get into places like Stewards, Leander Club and Remenham, You will need to have a pass or tag (usually a cardboard thingie on string which you can attach to your jacket's button hole) and some clubs can be very strict on displaying these so the old "get someone to walk out with two of three and get some more people in" ploy can fail – although later in the day they are less likely to check. Spend the day happily wandering along the course, persuading as many people as possible to buy you a drink at the extortionate prices, looking at the stunning ladies in dresses. You may well find yourself being thrown out of some clubs or enclosures for poor behaviour, but given some of the things that customarily go in the rowing fraternity (and importantly the sorority too) you will be hard pushed to get anyone to notice anything but the most overt acts of depravity.

Dress-code: Highest rating Blazer possible (Olympic medallist: good; Marks & Spencer: bad; suit: worse), tie, chinos and a boater (if you really, really must).

The Travelling Cad

There comes a time in every Cad's career when being elsewhere is desirable or possibly even advisable – consequently the Modern Cad needs to be able to travel in enviable style. Here are some ways to make it less tiresome.

Blagging an upgrade

All of these techniques have worked, but remember if first class or business is full, they are having a bad day or any other SNAFU comes along, there's nothing you can do – accept defeat with grace.

Whatever happens, be good-looking or at least well presented – the stewardesses get bored, like anyone else, so any eye candy for them is always a bonus. If you look like a grunge rocker from Seattle, you aren't going to get a thing, except possibly arrested – they will never upgrade someone who is not dressed smartly – almost all staff and relatives of staff who fly the jump seats with a particular airline are required to be well turned out – so should you be.

There are three opportunities to get upgraded on a flight:

- At Check-in
- At the Departure Gate
- On the Plane

At check-in

It is easier if you are a frequent flyer – they will regard you as a valuable customer, who has shown loyalty and therefore deserves a little extra consideration.

Risky: Slip a £50 or two into your ticket and ask if there's "Any room up front?" – saying "Up front" should indicate that you are in the know, a seasoned traveller, if not a member or former member of airline staff. With any luck the check-in clerk will recognise the incentive to make your flight a pleasant one and upgrade you accordingly – the key is to make it as subtle as possible and allow the greatest amount of room for the clerk to manoeuvre, so that they appear to be acting perfectly normally.

Less risky: You can always walk into the first class check-in line and ask how much an upgrade is, in the hope that they will avoid the paperwork and simply upgrade you for free, but frankly it is unlikely at this stage (see below) since there is no incentive for them to do so, and they can easily charge you the full price – which really isn't the point – so wait until you get on the plane. However, having walked up the first class line, you have at least avoided the queue and they may as well check you in anyway.

If you are lucky, you may get the "check at the departure gate and we'll see what we can do". Bingo.

However, if you are checking in late, they will only be concerned with getting the flight away on time, so forget it.

At the departure gate

There is no harm in asking and you should definitely do so if you have been given the nod by the check-in clerk and no-one has said anything yet. They can change your seat allocation and push you "up front" or upstairs, but again realise that they are doing you a favour, so be polite and charming.

On the plane

It is not well-known, but once you are on the plane you can often pay to be upgraded for a significant discount on a full ticket to either business or first class – they are already up in the air, so from the airline's point of view any extra revenue is always welcome. The cabin crew have the power to upgrade on the spot and will know definitively whether there is any space "up front". However, the cabin staff may not want to go through the hassle of dealing with the forms and the credit card transaction and simply upgrade you for free. And don't bother trying to justify the reasons why you deserve an upgrade – the only reason is that you are too cramped and want more space, which is fair enough. So be direct, polite ("Hi, sorry to bother you, but I'm really very cramped in here. I don't suppose you could tell me how much it would be to upgrade to a larger seat?") and, if possible good-looking, and the staff may do you a favour.

Entertainment:

Now that you have blagged your upgrade it is time to sit back, relax, enjoy the champagne and plan phase two of your flight: entertainment and I am not talking about the in-flight movie (which they have specially ruined for general consumption).

I mean the Hostesses. There are two principal fields of play:

On the plane

- Again ensure you're looking your best – as mentioned above the hostesses are often bored and will let each other know when a suitable candidate is on board - a good indicator is if you are asked anything trivial – "Anything else I can get you, sir?", "Another napkin sir?", "Some more water?"

- Avoid being a greaseball – like most attractive women, they have heard it all before, only more so since some male passengers seem to regard crass flirting with the air stewardesses as a perk included in the ticket price. So don't be overly demanding or a dick. However, be friendly, chatty and show you've got a sense of humour – you'll be on your way.

- Hostesses have an enviable lifestyle, especially those on long-haul – consequently, unless you look like a struggling underwear model, you will need to show you can afford to keep up – ostentatious shows of wealth are always a turn off, but a decent wardrobe, watch, suit and the well-deployed premier league credit card, will mark you as a man of means, style and distinction. Some might suggest buying the hostess a gift, but it seems a little desperate. It's as if you are compensating for your lack of personality by trying to buy your way into her pants – which, of course, you are, but you don't want it to be too obvious. Instead you might consider a duty-free gift (champagne is always good) to the cabin crew team for being so great at looking after you: This has the following benefits: demonstrates you have some wedge, doesn't single any one hostess out (see divide and conquer in ploys section), and so is non-threatening, but will make her want to stand out from the rest, plus it shows you have no ulterior motive since by the time duty free comes round you will be near the end of your flight and so what would be the point? The answer of course is that you are playing the long game and you aren't after a quickie in the loos (they have to do work after all). You are angling for a rendezvous later at their hotel, ideally at a crew party (let's face it, if your chosen hostess proves to be a non-runner, you have a chance with the others, who let's remember, you bought a present for earlier – what a nice chap)

- Choose your airline - If in doubt, when booking your flight, check the uniforms – it should give you a guide as to what sort of "culture" the airline has.

- Finally, while still on board, if a hostess likes you they will often give you extra drinks – so if the miniatures are popping up like Oddbins just made a delivery, you should consider yourself on alert. A well-timed business card with where you are staying (make sure it isn't somewhere too downmarket – Hostesses will know the best places and expect you to be staying there) and a number, or a discreet note on a napkin has often worked wonders.

At the airport arrivals gate

More difficult to pull off simply because of the pressure of time - Wait at the arrivals gate with a huge bunch of flowers – then when the stewardesses come out last, as they will, once all of the passengers have disembarked, go up and ask if that's all of them, and look downcast when they say sorry there's no one else – you have a big bunch of flowers so you are obviously a nice guy – explain that you had asked a girl to join you for one last chance get back together and she has obviously stood you up – give the second prettiest (see Cad-manship for why) stewardess the flowers since "I'd like someone to appreciate them" and then say "Oh well back to the [whatever hotel you have booked into]" – which of course happens to be the hotel or a hotel near the one hostesses are staying in – if you have any chance, this will be when the hostesses will let you arrange to meet up to "cheer you up" – hostesses are naturally compassionate and hospitable (especially with charming, wealthy, romantic men). It is crucial that you look disappointed, but not a complete loser – the hostesses must have in mind "what kind of idiot girl turns this great guy down – OK her loss, my gain" not "What a sad, desperate weiner"

Cad Style

"Elegance is good taste plus a dash of daring" - Carmel Snow

Introduction

Appearance is vital - often people will check out a man's shoes and watch, to see what kind of chap he is - polished, well cared for and stylish shoes, and an elegant expensive watch go a long way. Then again a studied but relaxed style appropriate to the circumstances and most importantly, the impression you wish to give, will also mark you out .

A wardrobe should match your mood and the circumstances- sporty when you just dropped into the club for a drink, smart when you have a business meeting and relaxed when entertaining.

One of the secrets to being a cad is controlling how caddish you are seen to be - An overly zealous hostess, or perhaps jealous host, can scupper the best laid plans of the Cad about town, by letting the cad out of the bag.

Therefore you should appear as you wish to be perceived - gentlemanly and elegant - with a hint of steel and mischief - plus any other attributes that suit your particular style of Cadmanship.

Use this section to build a wardrobe of elegance, your hide, if you wish, from which to lull your targets into a sense of security, observe their behaviour, and when you judge the time to be right, emerge to capture the lovely creature's heart.

Style Rules

There are certain rules to be observed to constructing the successful cad-hide:

Rule 1: Avoid fashion, stick to classics – as a man ages nothing is more pathetic than seeing him trying to affect a youthful demeanour – by the same token, a young man in an older man's suit, marks him out as a pretentious twit at best and a young fogey at worst (the former can be made to see the light, the latter is beyond redemption and may as well buy shares in a corduroy manufacturer immediately).

Rule 2: Simplicity – solid colours (black, charcoal, navy) in the main standbys of suits, jackets, trousers and outerwear are most versatile and can hide the ravages of the cad lifestyle – your shirts, ties, and accessories can be used to display individuality and verve.

Rule 3: Proportion – get to know your body shape and dress accordingly – Tall men with lean frames can wear double breasted suits – the shorter or more portly Cad should stick to single breasted suits and jackets to avoid looking like a cube, a club bouncer, or a blimp.

Rule 4: Watch and shoes – all women look at a man's shoes, and many, his watch – get these right and they imply not only style and taste, but individuality and character. They can also make up for deficiencies in other areas. As my dear old mother used to say "Shoes and beds: always get the best of each; if you're not in one you'll be in the other" What she didn't mention is that getting the former right, will increase your chances of having someone with you to appreciate the latter.

The Basic Cad Wardrobe

Well tailored suit

Dress2Kill have a superb range of styles and will provide you with excellent tailoring. Find them at www.dress2kill.co.uk

A dinner suit

Practically a Cad's dress uniform – Bond introduced himself to Sylvia Trench in one.

Black self-tie bow tie and black cummerbund

Never, ever use a clip on (leave them to estate agents and used car dealers), if you don't know why stop reading immediately. There is some debate about whether to deviate from the standard black bow tie/cummerbund theme – On the one hand it does show some individuality and stops people from wondering if you are a waiter, but it does seem like a bit of a desperate attention-seeking ploy – being stuck for conversation without a novelty waistcoat or bow tie is rather sad for anyone over the age of… actually, anyone – and as such is rather indiscriminate. Instead, the Cad at large chooses to draw attention to himself only when he wishes, being able to hide in plain sight as it were, only emerging when he judges the time to be right.

White Shirts

Always in high quality cotton with French Cuffs – TM Lewin have a very good range. Can double as a formal shirt for when you have had a run of black-tie events, have another to urgently gate-crash and the maid hasn't come for several days.

Formal overcoat

In Black or Navy: Three-quarter or full length as to taste and personal shape – note it should be large enough to accommodate a reasonable sized young lady, for when inclement weather presses in and your voluminous coatage offers a welcoming and thrilling refuge. She may even think you a gentleman. A word to the wise – while it is acceptable to drape a gentleman's jacket about a chilly maiden's shoulders, an overcoat should be shared since a) it will likely be rather heavy and large, smothering her and b) it will probably be bloody cold or wet, so no point trying to be all noble and catch cold (sneezing is not a winning ploy). These can be worn casually or with a suit – either way a full length one swishes nicely like a cape in the right circumstances and gets one into the right predatory mode.

Formal/Dress shirt

We generally favour a plain rather than wing collar (wings seem more suited to white tie and can otherwise make you look stiff and overly formal) and a Marcella front rather than pleats; it is easier to take care of and iron. Frilly formal shirts are solely reserved for fancy dress parties and my father.

Roll-neck jumpers

Cotton for the Summer and merino wool for Winter – colours are up to you, but in the absence of a girl advising, stick to classic blues, blacks and dark greys.

Crew-neck Jumpers

Get cashmere if you can, although a cotton or linen mix will do.

Raincoat

No hard and fast rules here except to say don't buy a typical belted trench-coat à la Humphrey Bogart – You just look like an American businessman or worse, someone who wants to look like one.

Cotton Pyjamas

Not for you, you idiot. Nobody wears pyjamas these days, we have duvets – it's for her: in case she stays over she can always borrow the top and there is hardly anything as sexy. Possibly useful if, heaven forbid, you have to go into hospital "Yes, well I did it skiing down the Weisshorn last week – bit nasty in the end, but you've got to try because it's there, don't you?"

Silk Dressing gown/smoking jacket

If you can carry it off without looking too Noel Coward, go for it - although the fauxmosexuals amongst you may already use this ruse to good effect.

Shoes

All shoes are to have leather soles (anything else and you look like you work with a name tag) and be of standard shape (no square or excessively pointed toes – you aren't a footballer).

Black Cap – lace up Oxfords – great for work, but can be worn with almost anything.

Loafers – in dark brown, ox-blood or black. Key items of casual wear, if only to allow for speedy dressing should the husband or boyfriend of your current paramour return unexpectedly, as some of the more inconsiderate so often do. Also for when there simply isn't enough time to undress slowly.

Chelsea Boots – Also fast to pull on and off – very handy for those impromptu exit moments and many acceptable examples – RM Williams, Church's or Trickers, even Russell and Bromley.

Care:

Suits: They need to rest between being worn, so have 5 if possible, so that you can rotate and no one suit gets worn more than once a week – at the very least let them rest for 48 hours between outings. Dry cleaning can eventually wear a suit down, so do not do so excessively.

Shoes: Learn to polish them properly – It will not only give you a better shine, but a zen-like sense of accomplishment if you're into that sort of thing.

Consumables: Every suit should carry the following – a handkerchief, a lighter, a packet of cigarettes, some sugar free chewing gum, a notebook and pen and sample sized bottle of your aftershave of choice.

Essential Cad kit – Accessories for your armoury

A good watch

Shapes, styles, designs – including diving types. You can find an excellent selection of unusual and distinctive watches for not too much money – obviously it helps if it is a real Rolex or Omega Seamaster, but we won't tell if you don't. Helps if you have a good story to back it up - A Cad we know well has a Tag Heuer Monaco which he complains tells awful time, but which he won it in a very satisfying game of Backgammon against a complete tosser. He also left with the guy's girlfriend.

A reliable black notebook

Breast pocket sized – not just for ladies' details, but to note down any number of little snippets of information that you will come across during your daily travels – a good wine merchant, a particularly good blend of Turkish cigarettes and where they can be ordered, the name of the concierge at Claridges, witty anecdotes for your memoirs and directions to a weekend house party – the list is endless, and a good notebook, proportionately valuable – I recommend Moleskines – available in a variety of sizes – check for your local stockist at www.moleskine.com/eng (it also has a rather good history of these vital accessories to the gentleman of adventure) – those thin pens that they use in the Mandarin Oriental Hotel in London are very good too and they don't seem to notice when they go missing when you've signed the bill (although at those prices it's tempting to think you might get a monogrammed one)

A Dunhill lighter

Elegant and superbly heavy - even if you don't smoke they look the business – useful for the Lighter Introduction Gambit. Generally avoid Zippos, unless you are on exercise.

Cufflinks, Shirt studs, Belt Buckle and Collar stiffeners

Silver works with everything, but make sure it doesn't clash with your watch. Look at www.CollarsandCuffs.co.uk for ideas. With collar stiffeners, no-one can see them, but you know they are there – it all adds up to conjuring the right attitude for which Cads are renowned.

Silver hip flask

A very handy piece of kit – not only does it mean you cannot be caught short without a drink should you, by unlucky mishap, be some distance from a bar; you are able to demonstrate to your fellow man your considered priorities in life, thus identifying quickly those kindred spirits with whom one may share a pleasant hour or two at the bar talking to the ladies, play a few hands of blackjack or even borrow some money from to alleviate some pressing gambling debts or other affairs of honour.

A cigarette case

Similarly to the hip flask, a cigarette case if engraved with a suitably mysterious endearment will win the approval and admiration of many.

Cad Cocktails

"Man, being reasonable, must get drunk; the best of life is but intoxication" - Lord Byron

Drinking is a skill and an important one - A cad ideally should never be more drunk that anyone else - depending on the company this may be more or less difficult.

Richard Burton "never met an interesting man, who didn't drink" and neither have we. In fact you should view with suspicion anyone who doesn't drink and occasionally get tight. After all what are they worried about happening?

The bar can be a minefield for the uninitiated - do you know your Cosmos from your Martinis? Your sauvignon blanc from your pinot grigio? And frankly if your aspiration in drinking is a 10 pint taste test between Fosters and Carlsberg you're in the wrong place.

For some of the best essays on drinking with style and swilling with distinction go to www.moderndrunkardmagazine.com.

However, the key to drinking is to know what you like and like what you drink. Don't become a flouncing wine snob in the hope of impressing Henrietta, whose father owns a vineyard or sink Cosmos with Victoria, just because she's seen one too many episodes of Sex and the City. Luckily, most people only think they know about drinking and their stories revolve around the holy drinker trinity of the First Taste of Booze ("I stole a bottle of cherry brandy and necked in the garden shed...", the One Epic Bender ("As we stood outside the burning strip joint ...") and the Worst Hangover Ever ("Honestly, I thought I was going to die..."). All are exaggerated and should not impress you.

Likewise most people's drinking "Truths" are, similarly, bollocks.

Black coffee – Giving a drunk person black coffee just gives you an awake drunk person.

Hair of the Dog – The "Hair of the dog that bit you" merely postpones the inevitable. You may be able to gently wean yourself off the booze over a period of time, but I'm guessing your boss won't appreciate this sort of self-medication in the morning sales meetings, after a weekend annihilating yourself.

Mothers Milk – Drinking milk after a skin-full won't sober you up, but it will give your vomit that nice cold milky texture.

"I'm a single malt man" – Sticking to just one type of alcohol is no guarantee that you won't see yourself off, especially if you have only one drinking speed; quaffing whisky at a beer pace is a recipe for disaster.

Talking crap – "I drank myself sober" - this is especially total bollocks - you may well feel you have reached a zen-like state of serenity and calm during which your faculties are enhanced and your thought processes are like quicksilver - "I'm better drunk!" you hear them cry - I'm afraid not; you've just started hallucinating - you're as a pissed as a badger and God help you in the morning.

However, the following are true:

1 Drinking on an empty stomach, after very little sleep or prolonged abstinence will make you feel more drunk than normal.

2 Drinking neat chilled spirits is always dangerous - if in doubt visit Troika in the Old Town Square in Tallinn, Estonia; order vodka served in the "traditional manner" and let me know where and, importantly, what day, you wake up.

3 Shots should only be undertaken in rapid succession under carefully controlled conditions - as a guide, 14 tequila slammers on a campsite in Del Rio, on the Mexican border in 1991, attempting to beat the camp record in order to impress the backpacking hottie across the room, only to end up being very ill and in bed with the campsite owner's large and mustachioed daughter (in that order) would be considered the wrong sort of conditions.

Damage Limitation

Preparation for an evening on the sauce, careful management of your intake and pre-emptive pre-bedtime measures, should mediate most of the worst excess. However, if you're anything like me, who'll drop everything for the sniff of a martini, such preparation is the stuff of fantasy and regret. Still for the more organized and restrained, damn you, try this:

1 Line your stomach before you go out; anything fatty will do, such as a pint of full fat milk

2 Slip a soda water, instead of a vodka tonic, into the mix every now and again

3 Drink 2 pints of water and pop two paracetemol before you hit the sack

Common Booze

Before you start tackling the exotica of Mojitos and Absinthe, get the basics embedded firmly in your own mind and don't be swayed by fashion or any moron with a bottle he brought back from some malaria-benighted backwater and as a cardinal rule: never, ever, under any circumstances, taste Unicum from Hungary - it is what they based the taste of Evil Itself on.

Beer

Not normally associated directly with a cad's adventures, but after a hot and hard day's cadding about town there's little more refreshing, than sipping a cold one. Similarly, after a bracing walk in the country, possibly having blown great big chunks out of it and the wildlife, a foaming mug of ale is the perfect vessel over which to relive your day. Beer, lager, stout, ale or anything else, simply enjoy it.

Wine

Jancis Robinson knows a thing or two about wine and once said "most so-called wine experts bring prejudices, not insights" and if I may say so, she's absolutely right - Apart from religion, there is little else that so promises the hope of sociability, but actually promotes division - between those that think they know and those that feel they don't. There are many excellent writers on this topic and I recommend you read as much as you can to arm yourself against the tide of wine bores and oeniphile snobs, whose bored girlfriends you should be looking to sweep from under their upturned noses. As a ready rule, if you are faced with a series of different wines start with the fizz, then the white, rose, red and finally dessert wines (unless you are eating foie gras, in which case, have the sauternes at the same time) cleaning the palate first and then letting the progressively stronger flavours build up.

Champagne

Ever since Dom Perignon first said "Come quickly! I'm drinking stars", sparkling wine has been a cracking way to start almost any venture, whether it is a maiden voyage, corporate takeover or simply breakfast. No matter what people tell you, real champagne only comes from France, but that's not to say there aren't some excellent sparkling wines out there. You can be better off buying half a case of excellent Prosecco, for instance, than bankrupting yourself on a couple of bottles of vintage 'poo. Generally, your fellow guests won't care and you might want to have an evening lasting longer than a single glass of overpriced branded nonsense aimed at certain investment bankers with more money than sense, who know the price of everything and value of nothing – just a thought.

Martinis

Martinis are an acquired taste to be sure and are very easy to make badly. Also ordering them can be fraught with danger - generally, the lower rent the establishment the worse the martini and the more opprobrium you get for ordering it. Ask for one in a Yates Fighting Pub and you'll probably get punched - ask for one in certain hotels and you'll get a warm welcome, a comfy chair and possibly a high-end prostitute aimed at you.

As Gilberto, formerly head barman at Dukes used to say "A martini is a-very much like a woman's breasts - one is not enough and three...is-a too many". Like them or loathe them, never underestimate them

Real Drinkers

Be careful though, because there are some for whom drinking has become more than a pastime. For whom a pint is never enough and sometimes neither is a barrel.

These are the real drinkers like Dean Martin who could observe, with a clarity many envy, that you aren't really drunk if you can lie on the floor without hanging on.

Their exploits are extolled in legend wherever men revel and quaff and include Oliver Reed, Richard Burton, Richard Harris and Peter O'Toole.

However there is a dark side to this revelry. While any feckless impoverished student can claim to be a boozer while sipping sweet cider at £1 a pint in the student union, this is mere flirtation with the devil. They are Quaffing-light until they swap top-shop t-shirts for a Mr Byrite suit to become "account executives".

No, for the real drinker, the relationship with booze is a mortal struggle, literally a fight to the death, for if they cannot kill the booze, it will surely kill them.

Cad Seduction

"Sometimes you meet a girl you want to take care of for the rest of her life… for a few years" - anon

Seduction is the cad's stock in trade and each will have find his own style.

Alfie-like cheeky cockney chancer? Ollie Reed-style bestial force of nature? or David Niven dapper rogue?

The cad may be a keen seducer for a number of years and having cadded about for long enough, choose to hand over the mantle to younger players, having found his Elspeth. Equally he may keep his hand in from time to time indulging the the odd technical or practical pull. Alternatively, he may dedicate himself to the ignoble pursuit considering it selfish to keep himself to only one woman.

Whichever route, you choose you should find something useful in these chapters.

- Rules and Field of Play
- Cad Crumpet-Classification Cube™
- Cadmanship

Rules and fields of play

In love a Modern Cad is not the ogre he is often made out to be. The characteristic of the Modern Cad is charm and without intelligence, charm is nothing - consequently the boorish drunken yob whose fumbling attempts to pull is not to be confused with the elegance and grace with which the Modern Cad romances.

Why is it then, with this bounty of abilities and good intentions, does the Modern Cad have such a bad reputation?

Put simply, the Modern Cad suffers from what we shall call the Groucho Marx Syndrome - he'd never join a club that would have him as a member - after all why would he? Where's the challenge? And he does get so very bored.

And lest we should forget, marriage these days, is not the land of milk and honey it once was. So what's a lusty chap to do...?

This section is divided into the following parts:

- The Seduction Ground Rules
- The Cad Continuum™
- Common Encounters
- Motivation

The Seduction Ground Rules

There are 5 rules that every Modern Cad should familiarise himself with:

Rule 1   Men do not seduce women, woman allow themselves to be seduced

Rule 2   Women are attracted to Status, Confidence and Humour in that order

Rule 3   Boyfriends (or husbands for that matter) are a detail… not an impediment

Rule 4   Seduction is a numbers game, failure is irrelevant, perseverance leads to success

Rule 5   Leave them wanting more, but Hell hath no fury like a woman left with nothing

Rule 1: Men do not seduce women, woman allow themselves to be seduced

Let's set the record straight - Women decide who they like the look of and start to send signals (more of these in Cad Communication) – not the other way round – by the time you are moving in to chat her up she will already have:

- spotted you
- decided whether she finds you attractive or not
- drawn her friends' attention to you
- discussed whether you are staying the night or having a drink thrown over you

If she is either attracted to you or not wholly repulsed (but wants some confirmation from her friends that you might be allowed to be seen in public together), she will then make you leap through some hoops to:

- test your resolve and see what you're made of,
- see if you buy your way into her evening, or
- actually have some charm

But the important part is that women decide who they like the look of, not you – Witness the pitiful plight of most modern men (unless they're Italian, possibly) who take a shine to a young lady and their plaintive little wails of "Why doesn't she like me?" or blustering nonsense of "didn't fancy her anyway". No mate. She didn't fancy you.

On a happier note, this works both ways – "why didn't he call?" she cries, to which her myriad harpy friends will provide her with an incoherent slew of pop-psychology ("he has commitment issues" or "he is emotionally stunted due to a lack of affection during childhood") gleaned from vacuous glossy magazines, and man-hating vitriol ("All men are bastards!" or "he's bound to be gay") borne of rejection and frustration, all of which avoid the simpler and more accurate reason that he probably didn't actually like her that much.

So, you need to increase a) your visibility and b) your appeal – and in both cases, that's where confidence comes in.

Carly Simon had it right – walk into the room like you're walking onto a yacht. Not with your head hung low, not slinking in like you don't belong, not arriving and making it seem more empty than before – let's face it Bond is a terrible spy because he cannot walk into a room without everyone realising that James fucking Bond just walked in, but the ladies do notice him.

And I don't mean cartwheel into the room in a Hawaian Shirt with your crotch on fire.

You don't need to actively draw attention to yourself – the confident man will always be noticed, because a) most people aren't that confident and will notice if you are, and b) society has a self-organising pecking order and once one person notices a confident person, they react accordingly, thereby increasing the pressure on others to do so, increasing the number who do, producing a ripple effect – look confident, people think you're confident, they treat you as if you are, you grow in confidence – any questions?

Rule 2: Women are attracted to Status, Confidence and Humour in that order

Status   Ever wondered why the guys on the School Rugby team, always pulled? Because their status as Alpha male is a tacit fact and endorsed by the society around them i.e., school – this continues into later life, and is manifested by the obsession with cars, job titles and money.

                 However as we get older other criteria become indicators of status. Who is the same schoolgirl, now 25, going to want to date? The helicopter flying millionaire CEO or his former school mate who stacks shelves in Tesco?

Confidence   Women constantly rate confidence as one of the most attractive qualities in a man and if you don't believe in yourself no-one else will – The whole world steps aside for the man who knows where he is going or to put it in a more Caddish way – "fake it, until you make it"

Humour   Remember the funny guy who always hung around the Jocks at school? They thought they allowed him to stay around because he made them feel smart and made them laugh – when in fact he was sleeping with their girlfriends behind their backs.

                 Michael Winner, the film director may not be the most physically attractive man in the world, but he has still seduced many many women – How? The money and fame may have something to do with it, but any man who is willing to pull on a stripy T-shirt and impersonate a bumble-bee bouncing off restaurant windows in public, is clearly perfectly comfortable with his self-image, has a sense of humour and deserves to get a shag.

Rule 3: Boyfriends (or husbands for that matter) are a detail... not an impediment

It is often this very realisation that has led Modern Cads be who they are – If we accept Shakespeare's immortal line: "Frailty thy name is woman" to be true, what man would be other than a Modern Cad? Some men however do not perceive reality as the Modern Cad does and I say good luck to him but he should beware of someday being handed his cuckold's horns.

Let's look at this real-life case study conducted in a restaurant – note that while it serves to illustrate this rule, the protagonist uses a number of techniques to achieve his aims.

Case study

This case-study covers the three basic phases of a random encounter:

Phase 1: Rapport and establishing common ground – don't wade in, establish the basis and vocabulary for the encounter

Phase 2: Flirtation – develop the theme and introduce some fun to the proceedings

Phase 3: Disengagement – do not outstay your welcome, control your exit and retain the initiative

Background

A pair of Modern Cads are having a quick lunch in an Italian restaurant – It so happens that the waitress is young, attractive and judging by her playful tone and frequency of visits it seems the two Modern Cads are the most interesting things to walk in all day.

The following is conducted in a light, friendly manner – conversation that is laboured, forced or cliché-ridden, will be at best tolerated and worst totally ignored (except possibly by the local constabulary)

Phase 1: Rapport and establishing common ground

Establishing rapport is key – asking questions is a perfectly acceptable way to make contact and, importantly, to get a feel for the kind of person this young lady is – are her answers playful, teasing or merely factual?

After a few questions it is permissible to ask for her name "Sorry [as if it was rude of you to forget to ask earlier]. I'm [MC 1#] and this is [MC 2#]" - offer your hand if it seems appropriate.

Then move onto other areas: "We're looking for a good bar - Where's good to go out around here?" "I'm here visiting my father in hospital and I wondered where's good to go out in the evening". "So you're a student, what are you studying?" – whatever the answer since the Modern Cad is a knowledgeable on a vast array of topics, he will be able to run with whatever response she comes up with. More questions should follow interspersed with snippets of information about the Modern Cad's own experiences in the field.

Phase 2: Flirtation

By now, food has been ordered and drinks are on the way, it is time to raise the temperature a little to see if she is actually interested or just a really good waitress – Flirtation is not something you can read about, you need to experiment and match your approach to your personality – so don't be afraid to experiment and don't be afraid of using non sequiters, e.g., despite the fact that you ordered two bottles of wine, don't worry about suggesting that she is trying to get you drunk – if she likes you that won't matter and it keeps things nice, light and playful.

The objective here is to raise the budding relationship to the point where she is expecting you to ask her out, or for her number- but crucially you must not do so at this stage.

Phase 3: Disengagement

Having establish rapport and flirted successfully, she will be considering if not actually expecting you to make a move, but to firmly embed this thought in her mind, you have to take away the possibility.

Making as if to go, the two Modern Cads say thank you and could we have the bill, and return to their private conversation, firmly giving the impression that playtime is over.

Having taken away the toy, the Modern Cad waits for the disappointment to kick in and just as the bill arrives, he asks:

"I'm going to be around for a few days and am free most of the time when I'm not visiting my father, so are you free for coffee in the next day or so?".

"I'm not sure my boyfriend would like that"

"Oh hey, look that's not what I meant - I don't want to get you in trouble with your other half. I'd be in trouble too for much the same reason – when I said coffee, I meant coffee – I could do with the company"

"Oh. Well OK"

"So, look why don't I text you to avoid upsetting your boyfriend?"

"Yes, that would probably be a good idea"

Coffee is organised, which opens up yet another opportunity, this time one-on-one, to build further on the rapport and take the seduction to another level.

The principle that all would be Modern Cads should understand is that the boyfriend was only introduced as a mental hurdle for her to get over, not you - she was looking for an excuse to meet you for coffee and is asking you to help out with her guilt issue. By establishing that:

a)   you're a decent guy visiting the sick in hospital,
b)   you have as much to lose by implying you have another half
c)   there is no hint of impropriety by explicitly stating that "coffee means coffee" and
d)   offering to back off by saying "I don't want to get you in trouble"

The Modern Cad has created an exception to the normal rule that you don't go for coffee with charming men behind your boyfriend's back.

However:

a)   What sick Father?
b)   What other half?
c)   Saying that the feathery, quacking, waddling thing is a biscuit, doesn't make it any less a duck; and,
d)   Sure… you don't want to get her in trouble.

Rule 4: Seduction is a numbers game, so don't worry about failure – persevere and you will succeed

Surprising as it may sound, every Modern Cad has been turned down. However the difference between the Modern Cad and the normal man, is that the Modern Cad brushes it off without a second thought (except possibly to modify his approach as necessary) and moves on. Most men when embarking on their seductive careers are so devastated by the first rejection or worse, paralysed by fear at the mere prospect of rejection, that they never make it out of the post room of the great corporation of Let's Get It On Inc. whereas the aspirant Modern Cad in training is heading for the boardroom, grabbing the keys to the executive bedroom on the way and taking that puppy Public.

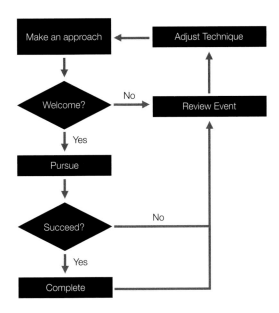

So don't worry about failure – easier said than done surely, but push through the fear and realise that it is entirely illusory.

Consider the following:

Women are people too

They have just the same hopes, fears and frailties as we do, only with more shoes and soft furnishings and fewer cars and martini glasses

They want to meet someone interesting and interested in them, someone who makes them feel special

The Sir Galahad Requirement – white charger, shiny armour, daring and brave, champion of truth, fidelity and honour – however while she is waiting for him to help old ladies across the road, and slay the "evil" dragon[2], she has no problem spending time with his thoroughly disreputable (but much more fun) cousin, Baron Malcoeur. With his midnight black steed, well-tailored jet black finery, wicked line in pillow talk and spectacular sexual technique gained from exotic maidens while carousing around Europe and the East, he is a more than diverting companion, as opposed to his dull-as- ditchwater cousin.

If she's not interested, why would you want to spend time with her anyway?

Trust me, you are a great guy. For a start you are reading this book. It is entirely her loss.

Enjoy the process

Much like counting the pennies, concentrate on her and what she's saying. As a result she will often succumb to the misguided impression that you are a really decent guy, interested in her as a person. Thus under the radar, you can really start to work.

Who cares if you fail?

Have you noticed how the only men who tease others for failing, never even attempt to meet women? Any man who has the balls to be in there, suffering the slings and arrows of outrageous denials will see you as a comrade-in-arms and knowingly nod, as he thrusts a well-earned martini into your hand, no matter how successful he himself is. Oh and by the way, anyone who brags about the number of conquests? Divide the number by 5 and safely assume he has very small privates. The successful don't need to brag.

Therefore be bold and do not fear that you may not succeed – at first you may fail, but you should simply re-assess and return to the fray. After time you will start to succeed and with this new found confidence your success rate will increase, thereby increasing your confidence still further – This ironically virtuous circle (see below) means that as your confidence and hit rate increases, you need make fewer and fewer advances until you instinctively know when you will succeed in a situation or not – reducing your failure rate to practically zero. There are many Modern Cads for whom a technical pull is enough, just to keep their hand in – they don't even bother to complete.

---

[2] Poor thing was only trying to get some sleep and some thieving bloody peasant chav is trying to have it away with his loot – so he turns a few into charcoal brickettes… and their families and villages – it's not a great loss to the gene pool, is it?

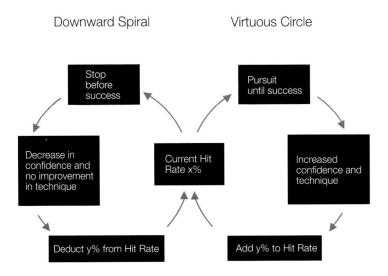

Conversely, giving up will diminish your confidence and reduce your success rate creating a downward spiral in which your ability to meet and seduce women will progressively diminish.

Therefore as you gain more experience your confidence will increase and also your seduction skills will improve, combining to increase your attractiveness:

Rule 5: Leave them wanting more, but Hell hath no fury like a woman left with nothing

By all means play hard to get and I assure you that this is a highly effective technique, but do make sure you satisfy her in at least one way – jewellery, a fabulous dinner, a thrilling ride in a sports car, spectacular multiple-orgasmic sex (although perhaps not all four in one evening. It can come across as a bit needy, desperate to please and frankly, you'll spoil her. You don't want her whining, "how come you never take me to Le Manoir in a Ferrari via Tiffanys and boff me till I pass out. . . anymore?" – it gets old so very quickly) – take your pick of these and many other pleasures that are within your gift, but always leave something on the table for later – a hint of even better times to come.

Therefore after or during your first encounter, sow the seeds of attraction and then back off. Piquing her interest and withdrawing demonstrates a number of things including your confidence, a matching lack of desperation, your valuable discretion and adds an air of mystery – "how can he walk away without so much as a kiss?"

This can work over a number of timescales such as during a date where you conversationally skirt the lust-laden topics at hand. You edge ever closer to practice rather than theory as the evening wears on without actually reaching the practical. Alternatively you can meet a girl for a drink, flirt a great deal, reach the coffee stage of the evening and then just as she asks you in, after you have given her all the hints that she should, you smile and say "Actually, I had better go" – leaving her on the doorstep – texting half an hour later to arrange a second date, after she's slumped on her sofa, calling her friends to conducting a post-mortem of the evening to see where she went wrong.

Conversely, such is the power and mystique of the Modern Cad that if a young lady, driven wild with lust, avarice, apprehension or celebrity-studded hunger, is abandoned, there is a strong possibility that she will commit some act of reprisal. This may take the form of spreading malicious rumours, acting frostily on your next visit or even more extreme forms of retaliation for this perceived slight - beware.

The Cad Continuum ™

Any relationship a Modern Cad has with a woman follows, to a greater or lesser degree, the Cad Continuum™. It has 6 phases and the more skilled a Modern Cad is, the more likely the activity will oscillate between phases 4 and 5 without ever reaching 6, until the Modern Cad intends the relationship to come to its regrettable, but inevitable end.

The Cad Continuum ™

1   Skirmishing and Reconnoitre
2   Encounter
3   Development/Honeymoon
4   Deviation and Discovery
5   Contrition, Repentance and Re-establishment
6   Ultimatum and Departure

1 Skirmishing and Reconnoitre

Prior to engaging your quarry the wise Modern Cad will have spent valuable time identifying potential avenues of approach, and mentally addressing the following questions:

What is her demeanour? (Happy? Shy? Confident?)

Is she part of a group, in a pair or on her own?

Is there a boyfriend or husband? Is he paying attention or wolfing around himself?

Is she part of your network of contacts (friends, relatives, work colleagues, bar staff, private detectives etc) and what can they tell you about her?

Have you met before? If so what can you learn from such encounters?

2 Encounter

Upon gathering all available intelligence, it is time to make contact.

Armed with the knowledge of your quarry you can arrange a meeting to suit your purposes – deliberately and overtly ("We should have a drink sometime"), casually ("Hi, my name is [ ]. So how do you know the host?") or "Accidentally" ("I was just out walking my rat and appear to be lost. I'm so sorry, I don't believe we've met")

3 Development/Honeymoon

You are now her new favourite pastime – everything is fresh and exciting and she is having the time of her life. She plainly adores you and you can do no wrong. During this phase you will build up the brownie points with which to fuel the continuum later. However be aware that you set the bar during this period – inundating her with flowers every Monday morning at work, taking her for weekends in the country every Friday and picking her up from the airport will only lead her to question you about it when you inevitably stop. So remember to factor in some unpredictability.

Work is always a good cover for not always being there and the more intriguing, high-powered and/or dangerous sounding, the better.

4 Deviation and Discovery

Now we come to the meat of the matter – the bloom is off the rose and the Modern Cad, being a Cad, is not monogamous - we explore the most common reasons for this elsewhere in the guide, but whatever the reasons, he will stray. This can manifest itself in being late for a date with her parents because of a simple flirtation with the cute hat-check girl at the Jazz club or being caught boffing your best friend's 18 year-old daughter who is staying with you in town, while she does some work experience – wherever it lies between or around these common enough accidents of fate, the Modern Cad will commit some indiscretion and whether it is the first or last he will eventually be called to task over it. The key is to have enjoyed yourself as much as possible while this phase subsists before discovery and be prepared to launch instantly into phase 5

5 Contrition, Repentance and Re-establishment

Assuming you have done your job properly earlier on, she will want you back; you just have to engineer your return to front line shagging as soon as possible. Having spent Phase 3 establishing a bank of goodwill you will also have taken note of certain facts:

1   Her favourite aspects of you
2   Her greatest insecurities
3   A list of her own misdemeanours

Having used this information to press the right buttons to get her feeling insecure and unsure of her own complicity in your misdemeanour, and having bedded it down with your bedroom credit rating, you then only need a plausible excuse, not for your actions, but to allow her to save face with her friends, family and conscience. The best ones are based on something she could have prevented, since she will in all likelihood be ready to blame herself anyway.

If the Modern Cad has kept the initiative sufficiently in his grasp, even fairly serious breaches of trust can be simply shrugged off since she will simply not allow herself believe you are at fault – "I shouldn't have insisted you meet my parents", "those knickers must be a pair of mine, which have shrunk two sizes and are a more expensive brand than I own which I must have forgotten he bought for me", or "My sister threw herself at you, why wouldn't she? You're gorgeous and she's jealous" – as much as anything else, having invested so much time, effort and emotion in the relationship she cannot afford to believe that she made so huge a mistake.

6 Ultimatum and Departure

All good things must come to an end and when they do the Modern Cad should be the one to bring things to a close, even if it seems that he isn't. It may be that you commit one breach of trust too many and you are given your marching orders (having monitored your relationship carefully you will know when this is coming up) or you have simply had enough and decided to call it a day. Exit strategies are set out later.

It is wise to keep an eye to your reputation and how the break-up will be viewed – in large cities, such as London, a reputation can be kept fairly well intact by moving on to other social circles for a while, whereas in more close-knit communities, the exit needs to be managed more carefully and PR consequences planned for and hedged against, to avoid being socially excluded – however if one has a strong enough social network this need not matter – your very caddishness will place you in demand and you can spin the break-up however you like.

Common Encounters

In terms of initial skirmishing there are three basic pairings that all Modern Cads should be aware of:

Encounter 1: Cad vs Cadette

Both parties are well aware of what is going on but, being well-brought up and game individuals, should not disclose this realisation – in fact one or other, or even both, may pretend to have not the faintest clue that a seduction is under way or their pivotal role in it.

Encounter 2: Cad vs Ingénue

The classic and some say still the best – the innocent naïve girl educated by the worldly-wise, older and charismatic male – the trouble is that it is so very difficult to find an innocent naïve girl these days, without getting arrested, so Modern Cads must make do with what they can and find a girl who is at least open to suggestion, keen to learn and, crucially, above the age of consent.

You should be aware that amongst all those of a non-professional status (I don't just mean those outside the profession of courtesan) in the seduction arena, there is a disturbing tendency to believe that the whirlwind adventure upon which they are about to embark is the start of a Something Beautiful. This can work to your advantage, since it has been well documented how much females are given to only providing the benefits of their ample charms, upon a sign of fealty and devotion (or failing that, a pair of Manolo Blahniks and a vat of Cosmopolitan). The fact that this is a temporary state of affairs is something you should not be so rude to point out. Too early on, at least.

Encounter 3: Ingenue vs Cad

There are occasions where the Modern Cad, by simple dint of his charm and charisma, unintentionally draws to him a young lady whom he has not been targeting (unlikely as it may seem) – she may have slipped under his radar in his initial sweep of the environment, or he may have been engaged elsewhere, on some other mission of caddish intent. Either way, the true Modern Cad is an opportunist at heart and therefore will have no trouble switching into primary caduction mode to reel the young lovely in.

Assuming she had passed due diligence, you should realise that a great deal of your ground work is already done, since she has made it clear that she is interested – (see Cad Communication for some of the relevant signs). Therefore you should waste no time in taking advantage of the situation and make your way together to a charming little bistro/bar/night club you know around the corner (reconnaissance is key, remember) where you can get to know each other better – or alternatively your abode (I leave it to the individual Modern Cad to judge when is appropriate to play the "Come up and see my etchings" gambit).

Motivation

Modern Cads should also have a working understanding of the primary motives of the parties. Self-knowledge is as important as knowledge of another, since while one allows us to encourage our new friends into the fissures of their own frailty, the other prevents us from falling into our own.

By understanding the motivation of his prey, the Modern Cad can provide scenarios, deploy gambits and simply encourage attitudes that act as a conduit for the particular motivation.

We have categorised them into three camps – those belonging to the Modern Cad, those belonging to the seductee and those shared by both, according to this table

Common to Both	Modern Cad	Seductee
Lust	Ego/ Force of Habit	Fortune and Trappings
Revenge	Nature	Mistaken identity
Humour/fun		Boredom
		Curiosity/Jealousy
		Love

1 Lust...

Anyone over the age of 13 should have a working knowledge of this one – if you don't, I for one am not about to start teaching you.

Warning: Blindness

Be very careful about being blinded by lust. Far more dangerous than donning beer-goggles (or martini-monocles, depending on your tipple of preference), the potentially adverse effects of this motivation are far from temporary. It has led too many a good Modern Cad, as well as ordinary fellows, to his nuptial doom. Usually deployed by a cunning wench with little more than a wonderbra and twenty-something nubility, soon to descend into post-thirty, genetically-irresistible swell, not to mention vast pants.

Warning: Expectation

Expectation can be a terrible thing so, if new to this pursuit, be sure to underplay and over-deliver rather than vice versa, until, ringing with endorsements, you are certain of your abilities.

Benefits: How old are you?

2 Revenge...

...is a dish best served cold, the sensible majority say. But the Modern Cad is not part of the sensible majority – he is part of a self-interested minority (of one) and will want to strike while the iron is hot, taking advantage of all the pent up aggression and avoiding all the sobbing. However, happily, the Modern Cad should not be concerned with long term yearnings or temperamental outbursts of the seductee directed at him, since he clearly has nothing whatsoever to do with what's going on (probably), so had better just shut up and get on with the job at hand. Then hail a cab and leave.

Warning: Complicity

Cunning being the watchword of the Modern Cad, direct involvement in nefariousness is to be avoided so have a care not to be tarred with the same brush – your public reputation should carry the general implication of misdemeanour, not specific details of your cuckold's horns dispensary. After all revenge is a two way street.

Benefit: Rules, schmules

These don't come along often, so grab them with both hands when you can since you may even be able to up the ante by suggesting she does things with you, that she didn't do with him to "really get back at him..." – have fun.

3 Humour/Fun...

Being up for fun and out to enjoy oneself is a heady motivator and is to be encouraged – the components of having fun should be emphasised enthusiastically at all times, "Yes, those knee length leather boots look great on you", "That plunging neckline is fab", "Hell it's the weekend, let's have another bottle and shots all round" .

Warnings: When the fun's over

Don't let a previously amusing dalliance turn serious – bail-out well before the fun ends and Daddy takes the T-Bird away.

Benefits: It's all in your mind

The right frame of mind is all that one needs and a true Modern Cad can conjure fun in the most dreary of settings, making it all the more seductive – anyone can have fun at Carnival in Rio, but a Modern Cad can have fun at an insurance seminar in Haslemere.

4 Ego/Force of habit...

Let's face it the attention of some young lovely is flattering to the ego and puts a spring in one's step – Alan Clark was renowned for his escapades and the joy he drew from the flattery. Similarly we often cannot help ourselves. Many a Modern Cad is an inveterate flirt and will turn on the charm whenever possible irrespective of our likelihood of success or the acceptability of the target – it is likely that these will grow up to be what is often referred to as a Roue.

Warnings: Indiscrimination

Charming an heiress is one thing. Charming the check-out girl (lovely as I am sure she may be) is another – the Ingenue vs Cad pairing is common and a Modern Cad may find attention from young, or even older ladies, whom he has not selected and would not, given the choice. Be sure to transmit focussed bursts of charm, and not simply broadcast all the time.

Warnings: Old fool syndrome

Sometimes Ego and Force of habit can lead to expensive evenings where the Modern Cad is taken advantage of, rather than the ingénue (or more likely the cadette), which clearly will not do. Too many men, past their sell by date, believe themselves blessed with a magnetic personality, capable of attracting women as well as they could in their youth. They slip into their old routines, believing themselves to be perennially effective, when in fact their platinum card is doing more talking than they are.

Benefits: The Technical

While a master gambler may carry a pack of cards with him to hone his card-counting skills or a mathematician set himself tough sums to solve in an idle moment, the Modern Cad can hone his art where he doesn't even intend to complete. The so-called "technical" is counted as a win. Some seductors are only interested in the score and lose interest in a seductee as soon as it is obvious they have them hooked – akin to an angler throwing the tiddlers back in. This is entirely acceptable, since it requires as much skill, and is, perhaps, all the more practical, since it avoids those difficult conversations in the morning, and is useful for passing the time while, say, waiting for a train or shopping with your girlfriend.

Benefits: Public declaration of intent...

By setting out your stall any young lady coming within range can expect to benefit from your attention. Thus a process of self-selection can present the Modern Cad with a stream of young ladies who are well aware of his reputation and therefore walk in willingly. See "Curiosity"

5 Nature

We are who we are – the route by which we reach the decision to live the life of the Vir Venustus is our own business. However it is safe to say that we are all driven by a dissatisfaction with the conventional role of ordinary compliant male and strive for a life less ordinary.

6 Fortune and Trappings

The desire to sleep one's way to the top is a well-known one and was practically designed with Modern Cads in mind. Similarly, offering a life of luxury and deceit can be equally seductive – just make sure it is discreetly handled.

Warning: Floodgates

Modern Cads should not let their indiscretions be broadly publicised - While initially flattering and rewarding, a deluge of attention can lead to unfair conclusions being drawn, when unrealistic expectation meets exhausted reality.

Benefits: Quid pro quo

The equation is a simple one as exemplified by the possibly anachronistic understanding in relation to Oxford May Ball tickets – sold principally as pairs, it was understood that should a lady accompanying a gentleman to such an event not be interested in pursuing the evening/morning after the ball has finished (or even during in some cases) then her half of the ticket is to her account, otherwise it is to his.

7 Mistaken identity (intentional or otherwise)

One or other party is labouring under a monumental misapprehension, which is fine so long as it is the one intended by the Modern Cad – if not, the Modern Cad must either decide to run with the scenario as far as he is able to discern what it is, or end the encounter immediately (exit techniques are discussed later in the Cadmanship section) – Charles Highway in Martin Amis' The Rachel Papers is a master at creating the intentional mistaken identity, but comes unstuck in the end - study his mistakes and learn.

Warnings: Discovery

The tricky bit of explaining who you really are and what you are doing there – survival here depends upon boldly stating that it was you who were duped, she is not who you thought she was and either laugh it off as you slip out or angrily storm off. Although it may come as a pleasant surprise and she may appreciate your consideration in not making her look foolish for mistaking you for someone else. Someone rich or virtuous, perhaps.

Benefits: Catch me if you can
Frank Abagnale – enough said.

8 Compassion

Sympathy and pity are poor reasons to go to bed with someone, if that someone is truly pitiable. If not and it's all a ploy, then it is an excellent and formidable weapon in the Modern Cad's armoury – unfinished poetry, a lingering broken heart, plaintive wailing about a family sadness – all good material – hints of an inner darkness are also good, but try not to overdo it.

9 Boredom

This is a common trick of cadettes – to feign disinterest to gauge the level of interest of the chap – if caught in the darkness of her indifference, it should be met with opposing and overwhelming disinterest, manifested in her less attractive, but more grateful friend or better yet, enemy (see divide and conquer and the contrived indifference ploy) – strictly speaking this situation should not even arise since you are in charge, you call the shots and no-one is disinterested in you, they are just people you haven't bothered to meet yet.

10 Curiosity/jealousy

The seductee knows you and your reputation – "I wonder what it would be like" they think, "How does he do it?", "what has he got that keep these women flocking to him?" – even if they don't and have heard of you from their friends, if they think they are up to scratch (say, an ingénue hoping to graduate to cadette) they may wish to sharpen their claws with the master. Here, kitty-kitty…

Be aware that sometimes curiosity can turn into jealousy – mild jealousy can be a good thing since it may goad them into action where they fear being usurped in your affections, but beware of bunny boilers of the "If I can't have him, no-one will" variety.

11 Love

Powerful and dangerous in the wrong hands, it ups the ante considerably and requires a delicate touch (and possibly a waiting aircraft or faked death) – taking advantage of the love motivation should be considered the nuclear weapon in the arsenal of Modern Cad techniques – yes, telling her you love her will probably get you laid, however take care not to be caught in the blast wave when the truth comes (falls)out.

Most effective on young ingénues and single women over the age of 30.

One is the triumph of hope over experience…

…and so is the other.

Cad Crumpet - Classification Cube™

The Cad Crumpet-Classification Cube™ allows you to recognise the roles adopted by different types of young lady - It is a strategic, rather than tactical device letting you know what manner of quarry you are hunting, leaving the choice of tactics to the individual Modern Cad to suit his particular "style of play" and the methodology of the lady playing the role.

You should be aware that as with life a lady's position in the CC-CC™ is dynamic. It may be that during the chase or the ensuing dalliance, the young lady's position in the cube will shift, often by dint of the Modern Cad's influence - the parameters of this metamorphosis are discussed below.

The three axes of the Cube are:

*   Attractiveness
*   Intelligence
*   Morals

THE CAD CRUMPET-CLASSIFICATION CUBE™

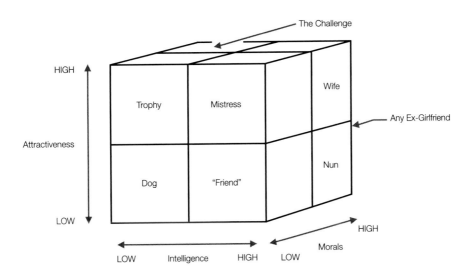

Attractiveness

Attractiveness is the most obvious criteria for assessing the fairer sex. However in these PC times it may not be the done thing to objectivise women and reduce their societal worth by simply determining their value according to the vagaries of individual taste, the oppressive yardstick of modern media stereotypes or how many martinis you have had - So that's why there are two other axes.

Also do not confuse attractiveness with simple beauty, important though it is. Attractiveness covers all of those individual factors which make up a more than pleasing whole: grace, style, demeanour, the sound of her laugh, the colour of her hair and the size of her trust fund, to name but a few.

A lady's attractiveness can alter as, for instance, whole new facets of her personality become apparent, whether through worthy discourse and charitable acts or simply expressing her penchant for Agent Provocateur underwear and chocolate body paint.

As a quick and non-exhaustive yardstick, award points for the following:

Aspect (scale)	Possible Considerations
Personality (1 – 10):	Charm, wit, generosity, vivacity, not being Welsh
Beauty (1 – 10)	Facial symmetry, flawlessness of skin, a killer figure and tumbledown locks of luscious hair a man could lose himself in for a week.
Social Skills (1-10)	Flirtatious chit-chat, coquettish body language, bar allure, telling their friends all about you
That... indefinable... something (1 – Heaven and back)	Well obviously it's indefinable, isn't it? Are you paying attention?

Intelligence

The quality of intelligence is often underestimated, but usually only by the unsophisticated consumer – the Modern Cad being a witty and brilliant fellow whose interest in a dull and boring companion will wane quickly.

Intelligence is the one factor that rarely changes. She is unlikely either to become a total airhead from being a rocket scientist, nor is a Model/Actress/Whatever likely to find a cure for cancer. Although changing hair colour between blonde and brunette may have an effect on how the young lady is treated depending on male assumptions .

Consider the following as a ready reckoner:

Aspect	Possible Considerations
General knowledge	Current affairs, the Arts, her boyfriend/husband's train-timetable
Education (Geoff, Attila, Desmond, Thora or Douglas)	Where, what, with whom and how much?
Conceptual Versatility	"If a martini before and a cigarette afterwards are the three best things is life, what are you doing later?"
Conversational dexterity	"Don't worry Darling, you work late - I'll just have one of the girls over to watch Casualty"

Morals

The attitude of a particular young lady to moral turpitude, to committing acts of breath-taking deception and generally living a life of luxury and deceit, have a fundamental bearing on the relationship with the Modern Cad. This is not to say that a set of high morals preclude the Modern Cad from pursuing a young lady. Quite the opposite, since this is the Modern Cad's forte – corrupting morals is practically the backbone of any Modern Cad's skill set and the greater the fall from grace, the greater the challenge and the polish to the sleek carapace of the Modern Cad's career [3].

Aspect	Possible Considerations
Self-Awareness	Ever taken the Purity Test?
Religious convictions	"So this "God" person… speaks to you, does he?"
Sexual history	How many, age virginity lost, same sex leanings and any corrective proclivities
Principles	Honesty, Integrity, Compassion, Never having anything to do with the legal profession

[3] Valmot's challenge in Les Liaisons Dangereuse was to seduce the highly moral Madame de Tourvel, break her heart and have her fall in love with him again – the height of the art and a textbook example of how to be a Cad. Apart from all the falling in love, death and other unpleasantness, obviously.

The 8 CC-CC Personality Types

1 *The Dog*

Doesn't need to be explained in too much detail – she's both unattractive and unintelligent, but will sleep with almost anyone – a woman for whom the only attraction you feel is gravitational - I would like to say that no Modern Cad has ever stooped so low, but that would be a lie and we're among friends – it goes without saying such encounters are to be minimised and kept as quiet as possible- you have a reputation to think of, you know.

2 *The "Friend"*

The Friend is a vital addition to any Modern Cad's group of acquaintances. First a little background. There was a time when no man and certainly no Cad would have a female friend – there were simply those he had seduced and the rest of the other men's wives. These days, modern woman, having been brought up on a diet of the anodyne whinging and naval gazing about true love of Bridget Jones and Ally bloody McBeal, the high-maintenance acquisitiveness of Sex and the City and L'Oreal Ads, and the too-many-freaks-not-enough-circuses, insecurity parades that are reality TV, they all expect to be understood, pampered and, Heaven forbid, listened to – whether they are attractive, intelligent and engaging or not.

Therefore to arm you with the intelligence needed to understand, or at least explain some of the more simple facets of modern female thinking, your female friend is invaluable. She will have an encyclopaedic knowledge of celebrity trivia, fashion gonkery and faddish trends (through devouring mountains of OK!, Hello, Marie Claire and Heat magazines). You may at one time have been lovers, but through mutual regard and a recognition of kindred spirits you have decided to be friends instead.

It should be made clear that the attractiveness score is only apparently low, due to the nature of the relationship – the "Friend" is often highly attractive but, relatively speaking, is no longer a potential target in the eyes of the Modern Cad , and therefore slides down the cube.

3 *The Trophy*

Not destined to last and unlikely to be terribly interested in any of your assets, except maybe your wallet or your ability to introduce her to wealthy or powerful people. However her gain in standing or gifts from you are balanced by the effect a pretty girl has on those that know you. You wouldn't want anyone to think you are taking this seriously, but the sex is likely to be spectacular.

4 *The Nun*

Not necessarily of any religious order (now there's a challenge), but every once in a while a smart, seemingly unattractive girl, with high morals, will come across your path– it may be that she is classic wallflower/ugly duckling who needs the hand of the Modern Cad to coax her out of her shell. Or she may genuinely be hopeless. Your call.

5/6 *The Mistress (Cadette) and The Wife*

Both similar in intelligence and attractiveness, they are two sides of the same coin, separated only by a band of gold that may symbolise everything or mean nothing.

One is still a full-blown cadette and the other perhaps a retired one, possibly ready for a recall to duty.

7 *The Challenge/ the Project/Ingenue*

The challenge is an interesting character type – pretty, highly moral, but in some way unaware and naïve – the innocent ingénue, who benefits from the hand of the master Modern Cad. Often initially apprehensive, they can blossom before your eyes.

8 *Any Ex girlfriend*

This is the slot reserved for any misguided female who has mistakenly concluded that a relationship with the Modern Cad is no longer viable and she would rather go back to her husband/boyfriend/dungaree wearing commune. Thankfully a rarity, it is also one of the very few examples of where a young lady may be downgraded in the intelligence stakes – I mean really how clever is she, if she doesn't appreciate the Modern Cad and all he has to offer? It should be acknowledged that the Modern Cad must bear some of the blame in this sorry situation, having usually failed to spot the tell-tale signs, e.g., insistence on introducing him to her friends, family and "this lovely little jeweller just off Hatton Garden". However we can put such things down to youthful exuberance and chalk it up to experience.

Cadmanship

Bond: "Why did you marry him?"

Paris Carver: "He said he loved me."

Bond: "Hmm, that always sounds good."

This section is divided into Techniques and Advanced Techniques and there is a further section devoted to Counter-Cadmanship, the dark art of female manipulation.

This is a broad topic that has been developed over centuries by true cads - a full understanding takes a lifetime of education and experience, but we have provided here an overview of some of the major techniques with which every self-respecting Modern Cad should be familiar.

The array of techniques, ploys, stratagems and gambits in this guide can be divided into the following broad categories:

- Direct techniques
- Oblique techniques
- Post-conquest/the game's afoot ploys
- Exit strategies
- Advanced Techniques
- Counter-Cadmanship

Direct techniques

These are concerned with the tactics of the battlefield and to be deployed as circumstances change – the Modern Cad is able to choose a technique that best suits his target, the environment and his own particular style of Caddery.

A) Give her the gift of missing you

It is well-known that absence makes the heart grow fonder and that familiarity breeds contempt – therefore be sure to cultivate fondness and banish contempt by ignoring her every once in a while. It really works wonders.

B) Begging back in

Having arsed something up you may be in need of a little help getting back into her good books – have no fear or embarrassment of implying your devotion if necessary – you needn't mean it and plainly your actions will speak eloquently enough to any one of your peers who may observe you deploying this technique – the following are a few useful phrases:

"Darling, I was wrong. I'm sorry. I love you." Simple. To the point. It gets the job done – the Ronseal of phrases, if you like.

"You're a darling little angel and you know I absolutely adore you" – slightly patronising, but often useful.

"Don't you love me any more?" Guilt – works wonders.

C) Contrived indifference

Using guerrilla tactics Modern Cads have adopted this technique from women - Feigning disinterest works with most women except the terminally self-absorbed and especially well with pretty girls who are used to attention – tell them you think them a little thin, that their bottoms are too small and that you like a girl you can have a conversation with.

D) Cockiness and humour

Dare to say what is on your mind – most men don't and think flattering the little darlings is the way into their hearts and other organs.

NO!

Women like a challenge as much as men and those used not to chasing, but being chased, love it all the more – challenge her point of view and then ignore her answer, you have better things to think about – again particularly good with very pretty girls ("How good a lover he must be, if he can afford to risk offending me?" They'll wonder) – less good with ugly girls, who will genuinely think you are being rude – which let's face it, you probably are.

So, challenge their views, be suggestive and rude, but deliver it with a smile and a joke, especially about them abusing men (this will make them justify themselves and gives you an excuse to wander, verbally at least, into their private lives) letting them feel they are in on a wicked joke.

Arrogance can also play a vital part.

"You'll call" you say with a saucy smile.

"How do you know?" she demands,

"Oh, I can just tell."

"You're very arrogant - you know that?", She says.

Then you know you have succeeded, since her comment on your arrogance is a sure fire sign she finds you attractive otherwise she'd simply walk away having told you where to stick your cocky attitude.

A friend of surprising charm and effectiveness has often succeeded due in no small part to his incredible apparent rudeness. When asked what he does for a living, he will often reply "You wouldn't understand". So shocked by this bold attack on a girl's intelligence she will often seek to prove him wrong, and thereby has already fallen into his trap.

E) Blatant up-front honesty

This is also touched on in the Cad Communication section but it speaks volumes for your confidence – no harm in asking, she can only say no, who dares wins, ask and ye shall receive - any number of clichés, sayings, mottos and pronouncements all say the same thing: Speak your mind.

So when reaching that crucial juncture of the evening when it can go one of two ways don't be afraid of answering the question "what are you thinking?" with "Well, I was thinking about taking you to bed". Similarly there is no harm in responding to "what do you look for in a woman?" with "Intelligence, beauty, charm and a marked enthusiasm for fellatio". No harm at all.

F) Overwhelming with details

This only really works with stupid girls.

G) Use of names

After engaging a young lovely in conversation in a bar ("Hi, I'm sorry. I don't believe we've met") use their name often and with authority – it will remind them of teachers in school or their parents and put you in charge. Especially if you use their first two names formally – so if they are call Jenny by their friends and their middle name is Anne – at certain points in the evening you will sternly refer to her as "young Jennifer-Anne" – she will feel like a naughty school girl and if you are lucky start playing the part...

H) Playing on insecurity

This can be about almost anything and applied to almost anyone, male or female.

Women: weight, looks, singledom in the face of advancing age, not being taken seriously, thinking themselves unattractive, social standing relative to friends standing close by, peers in the vicinity and all other women in general.

And don't just make the Girls insecure – any other poachers in the vicinity should be made to feel inadequate as soon as possible, so:

Men: Money, jobs, fitness, sporting prowess, success with ladies, sexual performance, height, where they are on the property ladder, driving.

I) Divide and conquer

Not necessarily literally, but separate one from the herd mentally so that they do not rely on the attitudes and assumptions of other competing females. Women think nothing of poisoning the chance of female friends, if they themselves have no chance of pulling – do not let her be influenced by their lack of imagination, unattractiveness or dungaree-wearing, Guardian-spouting feminista prejudices.

Instead ask for her help in getting drinks, if she wants to go outside for a cigarette or feels like dancing.

Also be prepared to comment on her peer's outfits, general appearance, intelligence or attitude. Here it is important to pick up on the subtle byplay between the ladies so that you know where the fault lines are – Faced with a loud attention-seeking member of a group of girls and her comment of "they're not wrinkles darling, they're laughter lines!" a paid-up Modern Cad comments sotto voce to the girls nearest him "Nothing's that fucking funny". Suddenly he is the newest member of their united front to destroy her.

J) Combine and conquer

A subtle but devastating and counter-intuitive technique, which leads nicely into the Nash Equilibrium Pull (see below). It is predicated on the basis that pretty girls will often spend their time with a less attractive friend - why this happens no-one really knows - is it:

Self-esteem?

Pretty Girl: "I'm prettier than her."

Less Attractive Girl: "She makes me look good",

Tactical?

PG: "I'll pass on all the unattractive guys to her."

LAG: "At least I get to meet men this way", or

Utterly selfish?

PG: "Her dungarees have pockets for my lippy" etc.

LAG: "One day she'll give up men and come to our side…"

For whatever reasons, if you go straight up to both of them and say "Hi, you must be sisters…" the pretty one will be stuck, as she won't want to comment on how her friend is way too mousy, shy or butch to be related and her friend will be thrilled, gaining you valuable brownie points.

K) Holding Back

Related to feigning disinterest, this is used during an encounter when you are relatively well advanced in your plan – having established rapport hold back a little and let her come to you. It not only reinforces your hold, but acts a useful check to make sure things are proceeding as they should.

L) Hilton Seclusion ploy (Divide and Conquer: variant b)

A bit specific, but can be applied to any tall building or seemingly inaccessible area – Head for the roof access at the Park Lane Hilton, London – from Windows on the World, turn right out of the lift, head to the stairwell and proceed to the top. There is roof access and the views are simply stunning – does get a bit breezy so employ the Siberian survival training technique and of course don't do this if you think you might be stupid or drunk enough to fall off...

As almost successfully used by James Bond in the Spy Who Loved Me – beware of stunning Russian spies who ask you to light their cigarettes.

Oblique techniques

Often overlooked these broader strategic weapons are used to establish mood, expectation and set up the target for exploitation via the direct techniques, which, while powerful in and of themselves are at their most effective in the context of the oblique arsenal.

A) Blagging your way in

"Don't worry they're with me" pointing to legitimate guests behind you as you guide your guest ahead. It is crucial to be utterly confidant.

B) Impressive shows of:

• *Physical skill/prowess/courage:*

It's primal and hardly subtle, but if you can carry it off, it's devastating, so learn to waterski, snow ski, sail, play rugby, scuba dive, race cars and, depending on your moral flexibility, kill people for a living.

• *Munificence*

If you run into some biddable fellow and a stunning girl he has, against all reason, managed to drag out with him get the maitre d' to place you at a decent table or the doorman to let you past the queue using your familiarity with the venue and then loudly state, that next time they be your guests, after all you've just been theirs – choose your audience carefully, but many English people will go, "Er but of course… not at all, er… my pleasure." You can then move in on the girl while he frets about the bill.

• *Knowledge*

This is of course a bluff. The important thing is to seem as if you know an enormous amount about a topic without actually having to go to the dreadful bother of really doing any work to learn it: one of the best openers is to start with: "The three most important things to realise about this topic are…" this implies that you have sifted through your encyclopaedic knowledge of whatever it is, considered all the issues carefully and concluded on these three points. Of course, you only know three issues and trot them out repeatedly. Given the chance, you should take the time to ask an expert in whatever field, who you happen to meet, what the top three issues/ points/ most important things in their field are, make a note of them and then store them for later. Most people will assume that if you can summarise a whole industry, academic subject or socio-political conundrum in three points, that you must be an expert in the field yourself.

• *Daring:*

A man should put his money where his mouth is – especially if he is constrained by that most debilitating of conditions: being English – we are taught to be mild, polite, never cause offence, never draw attention to ourselves and conduct ourselves with the utmost decorum – consequently when faced with these preconceptions, it is incredibly effective to blow them out of the water by being confidant, taking charge and indifferent to the stares, attention or amazement of the general public.

If you want to stand in a fountain in the middle of a crowded restaurant and deliver an exposition on the virtues of knitwear and the quality of heroism that compels a man plunge into a foaming river to save a solid gold baby (don't ask) or if you want to tango up the stairs in Quaglinos, taking a bow to applause from the enthralled diners, and use a handy nearby fellow as a cigar rest, do so.

The women will love you for it and the staff can only have you arrested.

Post-conquest/the game's afoot ploys

To ensure that the Modern Cad remains in control after the initial skirmishing is finished he will often use a range of ploys to keep matters skewed in his favour – things may turn against the Modern Cad either through his own misdemeanour (and the likely reporting of it, by some misguided simpleton or unsporting rival) or more likely simple effluxion of time – the Modern Cad is a busy chap and he cannot be expected to keep tabs on ephemera – therefore upon discovering he needs to engage in some light relationship tuning, the Modern Cad should reach for these tools.

A) Inconsistency

Being available and having a routine means you are predictable and therefore dull – she's here for a good time, not a long time, man – so vary your routine and surprise her – be unavailable when she calls or suggests something, but turn up at her flat with chocolate body paint and champagne at 2am, after she's had girls' night out. She'll be pissed off, pissed up and keen to make you pay – but above all grateful that you have proved all her doubting (but nevertheless completely correct) friends wrong. At least for now…

B) Female Superiority

Often it is to the Modern Cad's advantage to be found in the wrong. The target of your affection, if a feisty and strong-minded lady, will understandably feel at a disadvantage if she is constantly responding to your call. Therefore engineer a situation in which you may be criticised by her – this should not be taxing for most men, as we are always to blame for something it seems. Thereafter this will give her a misguided, but comforting sense of superiority. In this state of relaxation, when she feels all is well in the world and that she believes she is in charge, you will be able to have a reasonably rational discussion, during which questions are not automatically answered violently in the negative.

C) Jealousy – the Modern Cad's friend

This has been briefly touched upon before as a motivation, but there are subtleties to actually pressing it to your advantage. There may be times when a Modern Cad feels that he may be losing the attention of the lady in question.

This simple, but highly effective ploy plays upon natural female insecurity and their competitive natures.

Having already established what a great chum a stunning female friend of yours is (always good if a former girlfriend, see Appendices for anecdotal evidence) get her to come along to a group outing to a bar, restaurant or party and be sure to spend plenty of time flirting with her. Upon returning to your current inamorata, you will almost certainly be quizzed about your friendship ("She's very pretty - Did you say she was she was single?", "When did you break up?", "You two seemed very chatty"), which you lightly dismiss with "We're just friends", while looking fondly over at your chumette. Obviously she can't criticise you for:

A)   having a female friend; this is surely a good thing, showing you are not a macho blustering idiot, but a man of sensitivity; or,

B)   talking to her; you are friends after all and on what basis could she complain? – is she your girlfriend/wife?
         No, she is the one cooling off.

However she will become jealous and want to establish publicly her hold on you, by stepping up her own charm offensive. Ideally this will be with whispers of promised indiscretions involving ice-cubes, Altoids and Agent Provocateur underwear, if not immediately getting dragged into a bathroom cubicle for a quick…chat.

Exit strategies

Sometimes it's just got to end and no sensible chap should get into a situation as tricky as romantic entanglement without checking where the ejection handles are and how they work.

However, a man often stays his hand for a lack of the suitably worded exit strategy. Therefore consider the following approaches ranging in severity, depending on how gently the Modern Cad wishes to disappoint the dear lady, and that in turn often depends on whether a repeat fixture would be desirable.

(In increasing order of harshness)

Gambit 1a:	"it's not you, it's me. I just can't commit. You're lovely."
Gambit 1b:	"I'm just really messed up at the moment and kinda on the rebound, so don't want to lead you on...bye... no, really... leave now."
Gambit 2:	"I just don't think our communication has been going that well recently - perhaps we should just call it a day" (after not calling for 3 weeks).
Gambit 3:	"I just don't think this is going to work..." the morning after she does something drunkenly heinous while you were pouring this drinks.
Gambit 4	"Step forward all those in a relationship - as you were, Johnson [or whatever her surname is]."
Gambit 5	"I've met someone else."
Gambit 6	"It's not me, it's you."
Gambit 7	"Oh hi! Sorry let me cover up. We were just.... Have you met...? err...what was your name again? Oh how funny you share the same surname. Sisters? Really?Small world..."

Advanced techniques

Once a Modern Cad has mastered the basics he can graduate to more advanced techniques for the bolder, more confident Modern Cad, who has had time to season his abilities and is ready for great challenges.

There are many - we examine two here:

The Nash Equilibrium Pull and The Multiple Assignation Management System ™

The Nash Equilibrium Pull

Some of you may have heard of John Nash. Brilliant fellow. Nobel prize winner for Economics in 1994. Subject of a film with Russell Crowe called "A Brilliant Mind" – some trouble with schizophrenia, but who are we to judge? Anyway he came up with a brilliant theory called the Nash Equilibrium (bear with us now):

A Nash equilibrium is a set of strategies, one for each player, such that no player has incentive to unilaterally change his action. Players are in equilibrium if a change in strategies by any one of them would lead that player to earn less than if he remained with his current strategy.

To see this in action imagine this scenario:

You are amongst male chums in a bar and you spy a group of girls, all attractive, but there is a single girl who is by far the better looking.

What do you do?

Option 1: a group of you approach the most attractive female – immediately she is the scarce resource, has a choice of you all and only one, if any, will win her affections (and even this is unlikely to since she probably won't abandon her friends – assuming she is a good girl). Do you a pursue your original strategy with her and hope to be the one (odds against you)? Or do you change strategy and go for one of her less attractive friends, who will be annoyed at your choice of the obvious pretty one and decline your advances? Logic dictates that you stay in play for the attractive girl, since a change in your strategy now will lead to almost automatic failure, in the hope that she will succumb to your charms ahead of your fellows (frankly, unlikely). The Nash Equilibrium has trapped you.

Instead, consider this:

Option 2: Irrespective of your competitors' strategies, if you approach one (or all) of the less attractive friends you garner the following benefits over your fellows:

- The girls are flattered that you seemingly chose them and ignored the obvious pretty girl (you are not only a decent guy, but also "different" and "not like the rest").

- You can be the centre of attention leading the laughter and games, biding your time, deciding whether any of them takes your fancy.

- You become the scarce resource for the group of friends, and in a reversal of the normal status quo in a bar, they have the lower odds of pulling YOU and must therefore compete for YOUR attention.

- The group will endorse what a great guy you are amongst themselves and to the pretty one.

- The pretty girl will wonder why it is ALL of her friends are spending time laughing and having a great time with you, and why is she with this bunch of desperate losers?

Multiple Assignation Management System ™

Otherwise known as "living dangerously". Clearly, a talented and lusty Modern Cad may wish to have more than one target on the go at once – this is where the Multiple Assignation Management System ™ comes in, to manage some of the trickier aspects of this harmless pastime.

Issue 1 - Memory

The more astute among you will have noticed the obvious problem with having multiple nubile totties running around, all mistakenly thinking you are going out with them and them alone.

How are you supposed to remember all of their names?

Luckily Cad-kind has recognised this issue and the fact that some targets are apt to get testy if referred to by another girl's name.

The answer is a simply to call all of them "darling".

Issue 2 - Scheduling

Then there is but the trifling matter of scheduling them – again your trusty black notebook can come in very handy, however the Modern Cad is fully conversant with all forms of current IT. Microsoft Outlook has a number of superb features not least of which is the meeting conflict feature, which prevents any.

Issue 3 – Avoiding Embarrassing Overlaps

To avoid "accidents" when women have a tendency to jump to conclusions about which they get stroppy, you might wish to consider a few MAMS™ rules of thumb:

1   Always keep your notebook on you – It can act as a handy aide-memoire for when you update her particular section and discover some potential overlap with another lovely.

2   They should never meet – amusing as it may seem at the time, it is seldom a good idea to introduce one assignationette to another, unless the risk is low – e.g., they do not speak a common language or are "not the jealous sort" or the reward is particularly high – e.g., they can somehow benefit each other for which you derive exceptional brownie points or they may have compatible attitudes so that they can together benefit you…

3   They should not know each other or be closer than three degrees of separation – so that they need to be at closest a friend of a friend of a friend. Please see diagram below.

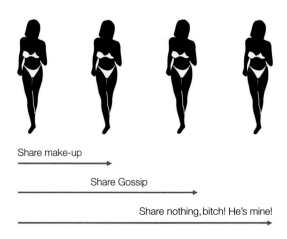

Share make-up

Share Gossip

Share nothing, bitch! He's mine!

4   Try to maintain a sensible geographic and socio-economic mix – an 18 year old student here, a 27 year old lawyer there etc

Issue 4 - Dealing with Disaster

However being a social sort, the Modern Cad will often find himself at venues where two or more of his inamorata are inadvertently in attendance. Furthermore there may be ex-girlfriends in the vicinity, whose existence may or may not be known to others or they may, themselves, be similarly in the dark.

How then is the poor Modern Cad to manage this situation?

First of all, to understand the problem, we need to understand the potential consequences - in the habit of women all over the world, they may speak, discuss common interests and surely as night follows day, amusingly discover they have the same boyfriend.

What ensues is known as the Los Alamos Effect – named after the story of how when the first nuclear test was about to be conducted during the Manhattan Project, the scientists laid bets on all sorts of possible outcomes, some desired (nice discrete bang, flashy but satisfying, effective and reached objectives) and some definitely undesirably (igniting the atmosphere of Earth, causing a catastrophic and unstoppable chain reaction which burned all life from the surface of the planet).

This is where the Modern Cad's chums come into play. Once a lone wolf, the Modern Cad these days recognises the need for male companionship and seldom more so than in this situation.

In any group a certain ratio of chums to each girlfriend/ex-girlfriend (counted the same) seems to be required to contain the effect – think of your friends as cooling rods absorbing all those spare electrons to prevent an uncontrollable chain reaction. This ratio however changes since unfortunately there is a network effect (yielded by the equation $x=n(n-1)$) based on the number of potential conversations each girlfriend can have with other girlfriends, so that as each new girlfriend arrives the effect rises exponentially.

Therefore the ratio is actually: number of chums to number of potential conversations –

Bearing in mind the following variables in your chums:

- Charm
- Good-looks
- Intellect
- Conversational dexterity
- Boredom threshold and
- Blood-alcohol level

And taking into account the propensity of some chums to enjoy stirring things up a little, years of highly scientific research and not a few martinis, has led Cad-kind to the conclusion that the best a Modern Cad can hope for is that a chum might be able to handle, to the nearest integer figure, the sum total of…

…..one…..

conversation with a potentially irate girl over a typical evening.

This yields the following table:

No. of GF/XGF	Poss. Conv.s	Av.conv per chum	Chums needed
1	0	1	0
2	2	1	2
3	6	1	6
4	12	1	12
5	20	1	20
10	90	1	90
15	210	1	210
20	380	1	380
25	600	1	600

Represented graphically we see the pernicious network effect at work:

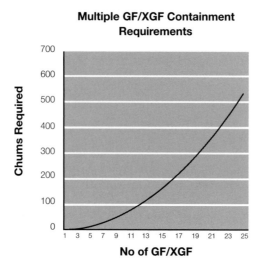

Multiple GF/XGF Containment Requirements

It is vitally important not to exceed (nXGF/nC)Max (represented by the curving line). At this point the number of adverse conversations exceed the system's capacity to cope and will lead to rapidly increasing numbers (that exponential effect again) of hostile women entering the party equation – this is not conducive to the Modern Cad enjoying himself...

As we can plainly see:

3 girlfriends/ex-girlfriends requires a minimum of 6 stalwart chums to fight off the forces of darkness

5 requires a, not inconsiderable, 20; and

15 requires a, frankly unfeasible, 210,

Which is a lot of drinks in anybody's book

No-one actually knows what happens over this number and the figures thereafter are purely theoretical.

Counter-Cadmanship

Women have techniques too - Learn to recognise these typical counter-cadman ploys:

Ploy	Response
Ignoring you	Make yourself irresistible by deploying Oblique Techniques and then ignore them right back
Being insensitive/rude e.g., "Who are you going to please with that...!?"	Brook no argument and be utterly confidant – e.g., "Me".
Criticising you – or treating a man like a project; a work in progress	We like living in our foliage-free flat with a vast array of electronic gadgets, drinking too much with our friends and running a wholly impractical car – she needs to go: any exit technique above 4.
Flirting with other men or your friends	Flirt with her friends more; sleep with one of them, then blame it on her
Putting the ball in your court e.g. saying something like "Give me a call"	Do so from a yacht, grand prix or ski-slope, have a female friend giggle in the background and pop the cork of some fizz – end the call quickly with "Sorry darling. Gotta go – give you a call sometime…"
Being unavailable e.g., "Sorry, I'm washing my hair"	Let it be known you took one of her rivals to any favourite event/venue of hers
Outrageous requests for gifts	Establish very clearly what the terms of the exchange are – if met with any variation on "I'm worth it" say "Really? Prove it"
Stubborn refusal to do what you say	Adopt a parent-child demeanour "All this whining makes me think you've been very spoiled…goodbye"
Flattery e.g., "everyone loves your voice, your eyes etc" or **Apparent Leniency** e.g., "you stay in darling. You don't have to come over", or "you have a night out with the boys	No real response needed but just be on your guard – she wants or is up to something
No-gift for you ploy – "I don't bother with gifts for Christmas/birthdays/Valentine's day. It's all so commercial" She gets you a card, but woe betide you if you fail to buy anything for her	Public and hearty agreement – followed by "Instead I prefer to make a donation to my favourite charity – I'm glad you feel the same" – Face it, you weren't going to get a thing and anyway, your favourite charity is you.

Appendix: Drinks for the Dastardly

Cosmopolitan

This is a very popular drink, especially with the ladies. It is fairly tart and quite refreshing, like many girls.

    4 parts Citron Vodka
    2 parts Cointreau or Triple Sec
    1 part Lime juice (preferably fresh)
    2 parts Cranberry juice
    Shake and strain into a chilled cocktail glass.
    Garnish with a lime wedge.

Bellini

    5 parts Chilled Champagne,
    1 part Fresh Peach Puree, Nectar or Peach Schnapps
    Pour over peach in a Champagne Flute

Bloody Mary

Hair of the dog – kind of like food – it's basically cold tomato soup with some added vodka fun – experiment to taste.

    1 pint of vodka
    3 pints tomato juice
    2 lemons
    3 tsps Worcestershire sauce
    2 tsps tabasco sauce
    Generous tsps of celery salt and freshly-ground black pepper
    Pour the vodka into a jug and fill up with the tomato juice.
    Cut one and half lemons into quarters, squeeze and drop in.
    Add tabasco sauce and celery salt
    Squeeze the remaining lemon half in but discard
    Taste and season
    Pop in the fridge to chill.
    Just before serving, add a couple of ice cubes.
    Also for an extra twist, serve with a jug of freshly squeezed lemon juice.

Bloody Maria

1 1/2 oz. Tequila,
Dashes of Worcestershire, Tabasco, Salt, Pepper & Lime juice,
Tomato juice to fill
Build in above order in a Tall glass, Garnish with a Celery stalk, Lime wedge & Jalepeno pepper if desired

Brandy Alexander

Dark Creme de Cacao to Brandy, Cream – ratio 1:1
Blend with ice,
Strain into a Flute,
Garnish with a sprinkle of nutmeg

Blow Job

Equal parts of Kahlua, Baileys & Vodka
Layer into a pony or shot glass
Top with whipped cream
This drink is taken in one gulp without the use of hands.

Sex on the beach

1 oz. Vodka
3/4 oz. each: Chambord & Peach Schnapps
Splashes of Pineapple, Orange and Cranberry juices
Shake with ice & serve in a Collins or decorative glass

Sex with an alligator

I am not sure where this drink originated, but it is a very popular shooter in Florida. It is a takeoff of the popular cocktail, Sex on the Beach and is just as tasty and fruity. This is aptly named as it will bite like an alligator or have you wondering just what you did while drinking them last night. The Jagermeister gives it just a little snap without the full Jagermeister flavour.

Equal parts of Midori, Malibu rum and Pineapple juice
Shake and strain into a chilled cocktail glass
Drop a drizzle of Chambord & let fall to the bottom of the glass
Float a thin layer of Jagermeister on top

Tequila Fun

Tequila is a strange spirit and not to be approached unawares; likewise its cousin Mescal. It can be ingested in a number of unpleasant ways, but here are some of the better ones:

Tequila Slammer

Shot of tequila
Slice of lime
Salt cellar
Lick flesh of "off" hand, between first knuckle and thumb
Pour on salt
Prepare self
Quickly lick the salt, slam the tequila back and then savage the lime.

Add a splash of 7up or decent lemonade to tequila in a larger glass and slam the glass down first, hand on top to get a more professional buzz.

Tequila stuntman

This is not for the faint hearted and we can't actually recommend you do this. God only knows why you would want to, but it's fun watching other people do it.

Same as before, except you:

snort the salt in a line (much like Peruvian marching powder),
slam the tequila
squeeze the lime in your eye.

Body Slammers

Much more fun than the previous masochism, for this you need a partner of the opposite sex.

The salt is poured onto a suitably moistened area of flesh, and licked off
The tequila is poured into and drunk out of suitable "receptacles", (just behind the clavicle, between the breasts, mouth to mouth – you get the picture)
The lime is held between the teeth of one protagonist and the other starts with a kiss, then strips the flesh off the fruit…

Repeat until you fall over or are overcome by more primal urges

Bucks Fizz

Dry champagne,
Freshly squeezed orange juice to taste ("No, really, it has hardly any alcohol in it at all…")

Champagne Cocktail

Dash of Bitters
Simple Syrup
Chilled Champagne
Put dashes in Champagne glass,
Fill with Champagne,
Garnish with a twist
Add Brandy to taste

Gibson

Gin or Vodka, Dash of Dry Vermouth
Stir with ice
Strain into a chilled cocktail glass
Garnish with skewered cocktail onions,
Omit or reduce vermouth if ordered dry

Kir

Creme de Cassis,
White Wine
Pour a healthy splash of creme de Cassis in bottom of Wine glass, Top up with wine, Garnish with a twist

Kir Royale as Imperial

Kir royale 3/4 oz.
Creme de Cassis,
Champagne
Pour Creme de Cassis in bottom of Wine glass or flute
Fill with champagne
Garnish with a twist

Mai tai

3 parts Dark Rum to 1 part each of
Orange Curacao, creme de noyaux and lime juice
Dash of Grenadine if desired
Shake with ice & serve in a Hurricane or decorative glass
Or add extra juice & blend with crushed ice for a frozen variation,
Garnish with a flag (an orange slice and cherry skewered

Manhattan

"Lord deliver me from those who know the difference between "shall" and "will", but don't know the difference between a Manhattan and a Martini".

Whiskey or Bourbon – to the ratio 2:1
Sweet Vermouth,
Dash of Bitters (if desired)
Build in a rocks glass or Stir over ice
Strain into a chilled cocktail glass to serve up,
Garnish with a Cherry,

Perfect Manhattan

As per previous but:

> Use equal parts of sweet & dry vermouth
> Garnish with a Lemon twist

Martini - Standard

> Gin – ratio of 4:1 or higher
> Vermouth
> Stir over ice & Serve on the rocks or Strain into a chilled cocktail glass,
> Garnish with a spear of Olives

Martini - Dry

As above but reduce vermouth to taste (some purists insist on only a few drops of vermouth ("so dry I want to be able to blow the dust off it") - this time garnish with a Twist.

Vodka Martini

Substitute Vodka for Gin – but you knew that right?

Mojito

> 1 1/4 oz. Rum,
> Splash of Soda,
> Dash of Simple Syrup,
> Mint
> Muddle Mint leaves with Simple Syrup,
> Add ice,
> Add Rum
> top with Soda, Garnish with a Sprig of fresh mint

Caiphirina

1 Lime
2 Brown Sugar Cubes
2 Shots Cachaça
Mix into a pestle and mortar and build over cracked ice

Add a dash of Cachaça to the Limes and Sugar before you muddle.

Pimms

Standard Cocktail

The great thing about it is that you don't even have to be half sober to make it – just stick it all in a large jug. Then add a balmy summer's evening, a punt and a number of girls in floaty summer dresses.

To make a 3.5 pints jug (just over two litres)

Pimms- 50 cl
Lemonade -150 cl
Gin- 15 cl
Apple-1 sliced
Orange- 1 sliced
Lemon- 1 sliced
Celery- 2 stick chopped finely
Cucumber- 10 slices quartered
Mint- 1 stalk

All other fruit such as nectarines, strawberries, cherries, kiwi etc can be added to taste

Pimms Royale

As above
Top up with Champagne